SPRING-BLOOMING
BULBS

An A to Z Guide to Classic and
Unusual Bulbs for Your Spring Garden

Beth Hanson-Editor

Janet Marinelli
SERIES EDITOR

Sigrun Wolff Saphire
SENIOR EDITOR

Mark C. Tebbitt
SCIENCE EDITOR

Leah Kalotay
ART DIRECTOR

Steven Clemants
VICE-PRESIDENT, SCIENCE & PUBLICATIONS

Judith D. Zuk
PRESIDENT

Elizabeth Scholtz
DIRECTOR EMERITUS

Handbook #173
Copyright © 2002 by Brooklyn Botanic Garden, Inc.
Handbooks in the *21st-Century Gardening Series,* formerly *Plants & Gardens,*
are published quarterly at 1000 Washington Ave., Brooklyn, NY 11225.
Subscription included in Brooklyn Botanic Garden subscriber membership dues ($35.00 per year).
ISBN # 1-889538-54-X
Printed by Science Press, a division of the Mack Printing Group.
Printed on recycled paper.

**Previous page: A classic spring garden scene features daffodils,
Virginia bluebells, and phlox.**

SPRING-BLOOMING BULBS
Table of Contents

VENTURING BEYOND THE FAMILIAR:

Classic and Unusual Bulbs for Your Spring Garden

BETH HANSON

y coincidence, it's early spring as I wrap up this book, and this year I'm especially attuned to the earth's reawakening. Although the overall mood of winter persists, with gray skies and barren leafless trees, I've already spotted hillsides blushing purple with crocus, daffodil stems poking through the brown leaves, and in protected spots the pale buds of hyacinths and the undulating leaves of tulips pushing up to the sun.

Like fluffy chicks, chocolate bunnies, and Easter bonnets, the appearance of these bulbs is so often cited as the signal that spring has returned that they have entered the realm of, well, cliché. These tried-and-true spring-blooming bulbs are members of a large and diverse group of plants called geophytes—corms, tubers, rhizomes, and true bulbs—all plants that have evolved underground parts to store the energy they need to reemerge when the weather warms. Like its companion volume, *Summer-Blooming Bulbs*, this handbook is an invitation to gardeners across the continent to venture beyond the familiar and explore this wide-ranging group of plants.

The heart of this book is an encyclopedia of spring-blooming bulbs in which about 50 spring beauties, from the beloved to the unusual, are profiled. No matter where you live, you will find bulbs that will thrive in your garden. Consult this section to learn about the cultural needs of each plant and how best to offset its individual attributes by combining it with other bulbs, perennials, annuals, shrubs, and trees. Elsewhere in these pages you will dig into the biology of bulbs, learn techniques for growing spring bloomers in containers, read about natural pest and disease controls for these plants, and more.

Plant a variety of spring-blooming bulbs in the fall and they will delight you from the bleak days of late winter to the onset of summer.

Deciduous forests are the home of North American painted trillium, *Trillium undulatum*. Like other woodland bulbs, trilliums emerge before the trees leaf out, taking advantage of the light reaching the forest floor.

It's important to note here that the search for the new and unusual can have unintended consequences. Hundreds of thousands of bulbs are collected in the wild each year and sold to the nursery trade, and in the process natural populations of bulbs are depleted and pushed to the brink of extinction. However, it is possible to enjoy these charming plants in our gardens and ensure their survival in their natural habitats. The Chilean blue crocus, *Tecophilaea cyanocrocus,* for example, is one bulb that gardeneres have helped save from extinction. It is believed to have disappeared altogether from its native habitat, temperate grasslands near Santiago, Chile, and to survive only in small numbers in gardeners' greenhouses and plots. Biologists have devised a plan to propagate the Chilean blue crocus using this horticultural stock and reintroduce it to its former habitat. See "Buyer Beware: A Gardener's Guide to Bulb Conservation," page 14, for important information on buying bulbs.

Tulips have been in cultivation for centuries, with hybridizers competing to come up with ever showier varieties in ever changing colors. Above, the purplish tulip cultivar 'Negrita' combines with the pink blooms of 'Magier'.

Tough, vigorous, disease-resistant, and beautiful, heirloom bulbs, such as *Crocus vernus* 'King of Striped', above, are adaptable to many garden situations. Unfortunately, many are becoming hard to find and are in danger of being lost forever.

BOTANICAL SURVIVALISTS:
The Underground Life of Bulbous Plants

MARK C. TEBBITT

Crocuses and other spring-flowering bulbs owe much of their charm to their predictable and well-timed emergence from the ground each spring and to their equally convenient retreat back into it in the summer. Learning about why bulbs behave this way and what happens inside them during this cyclical pattern of growth can provide valuable clues to their successful cultivation.

The term "bulb" is widely defined here to include all those plants that have swollen storage organs at or below ground level that produce new leaves and flowers each spring. This definition includes the true bulbs, which are formed from swollen, modified leaves, as well as the bulb look-alikes—corms, rhizomes, tubers, and tuberous roots—which are formed from modified stems or roots. Although there are differences among these organs, gardeners refer to them collectively as "bulbs" because they have similar growth cycles and cultural requirements.

Becoming Bulbous

When the first flowering plants encountered regions of the earth with alternating wet and dry seasons, they evolved a variety of means for storing energy and water underground; that's how true bulbs, rhizomes, corms, tubers, and tuberous roots arose. As some methods of storing energy underground were easier to arrive at and more efficient than others, the same means of storage evolved independently in unrelated species. The distantly related primrose and begonia families both include species with tubers, for example: hardy, or winter, cycla-

Adapting to life in regions with alternating dry and wet seasons, some plants, such as *Crocus biflorus*, opposite, developed a variety of means for storing energy and water underground. That's how true bulbs, rhizomes, corms, tubers, and tuberous roots developed.

Bulbs come in many sizes. Top left to right: *Narcissus* 'Jetfire', *Hyacinthus* 'Blue Jacket', *Tulipa* 'Queen of the Night'. Middle left to right: *Muscari latifolium, Tulipa tarda, Allium aflatunense.* Front: *Anemone blanda, Crocus sieberi* subsp. *sublimis.*

men, *Cyclamen coum,* in the Primulaceae, and tuberous begonia, *Begonia froebelii,* in the Begoniaceae.

Certain early bulbous species were very successful at adapting to climates with alternating wet and dry seasons, and in time they gave rise to new species that colonized other regions with similar climates. Today, the three largest and most widespread of these species groups are known as the lily, amaryllis, and iris families. As bulbous species such as these continue to occupy habitats their ancestors probably first colonized about 35 million years ago, their way of life represents one of the most successful strategies found in the plant kingdom.

A Year in the Life of a Bulb

When you plant spring-flowering bulbs in the fall you are effectively planting conveniently packaged mini-plants. Cut a daffodil bulb down the center, and you will find fully developed flower and leaf buds that are just waiting for spring. Once spring arrives the buds expand and emerge from the soil, and leaves and flower unfurl. As soon as the flower wilts, the fully expanded leaves start to replenish the bulb's energy supply and a new miniature plant begins to form.

In the interest of next year's bulb display, it's important to allow the leaves to mature and photosynthesize until they begin to wither. Resist the temptation to remove or cover the leaves, even if they look messy for a few weeks. Do remove any faded flowers, though, as this will keep the plants from "wasting" energy on ripening seed and instead allocate this energy to the formation of next year's flower buds.

Even after bulbs retreat below ground, the flower and leaf buds continue to develop. Their final development is only completed after certain environmental requirements are met. Many spring-flowering bulbs come from regions with cold winters and must be triggered into flower by a period of chilling followed by an increase in temperature. This requirement allows bulbs to time their emergence from the soil to coincide with the arrival of spring. It also keeps them from emerging prematurely during an unseasonably warm spell in winter when their buds could be damaged by returning frost and any flowers tricked into opening would be visited by few pollinators.

Many spring-flowering bulbs, such as daffodils, come from regions with cold winters and must be triggered into flowering by a period of cold followed by an increase in temperature.

Where Wild Bulbs Grow

Most of the world's bulbous species are concentrated in regions of the world with alternating wet and dry seasons. In many of these areas, forest fires are common during the dry season. Bulbous plants are adapted to these difficult climatic conditions because their fleshy bulbs, rich in stored energy and water, can remain safely below ground until more favorable conditions arrive. Their stored energy and water reserves not only allow them to wait out an unfavorable season but also enable them to burst into growth as soon as the wet season arrives, giving them a competitive advantage over other plants.

Not all bulbs from regions with wet and dry seasons flower in spring, however. Some regions, like the monsoon-drenched Himalayas, experience plentiful summer rainfall and winter drought and are home to bulbs that are adapted to flower during the favorable summer months. The stately Himalayan lily (*Cardiocrinum giganteum*) is one such plant.

Two areas particularly rich in spring-flowering bulbs are the Western Cape of South Africa and the region stretching from the Mediterranean to central Asia. While the Western Cape is home to more species of spring-flowering bulbs than any other region in the world, most of these are treated as summer- or fall-blooming bulbs in our gardens since they are not hardy in most regions of North America. Popular examples include *Agapanthus, Gladiolus,* and *Ixia.* Spring-flowering bulbs from the Mediterranean and central Asia are better adjusted to the temperate regions of North America and flower during the spring in our gardens. Cultivated examples are numerous and include spring-blooming crocuses, irises, narcissus, and tulips.

Many central Asian bulbs, including certain species of tulips and fritillaries (*Fritillaria*), experience both hot summers and cold winters in their native habitats and consequently require baking summer temperatures as well as winter cold to stimulate flower-bud formation. In northerly gardens where summers are cool, these plants resent being surrounded by perennials that shade the soil above their bulbs during the summer since this cools them and keeps them

SURVIVAL STRATEGIES

Bulbs are reduced stems bearing modified fleshy leaves and one or more flower buds. Individual bulbs survive for several years and give rise to new bulbs from their disklike basal stems. Onions (*Allium*) and daffodils (*Narcissus*) are examples of true bulbs.

Corms are solid, vertical underground stems that usually have a thin outer covering of papery leaves. Each year after flowering, the existing corm is replaced by a new one that develops on top of it. Crocuses are corms.

Rhizomes are swollen stems lying horizontally at or below ground level. Irises grow from rhizomes.

Tubers are the swollen ends of certain underground stems. Hardy cyclamens arise from tubers.

Tuberous roots are the swollen parts of certain roots. Virginia bluebells have tuberous roots.

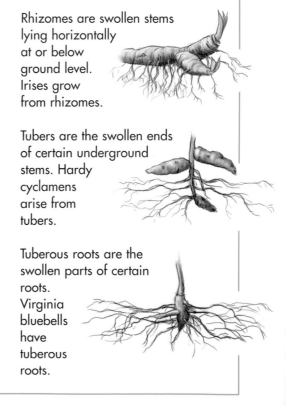

from developing properly. Conversely, in many southern gardens these bulbs are reluctant to flower as winter temperatures rarely remain cold long enough to stimulate flowering.

Spring-flowering woodland bulbs, such as the toothworts (*Cardamine,* syn. *Dentaria*) and wake robins (*Trillium*) of North America and the bluebells (*Hyacinthoides*) of western Europe, appear to be exceptions to the general rule that bulbs usually originate in climates with marked wet and dry seasons. Nevertheless, seasonal differences in water availability do control the bulbous lives of these plants. Woodland bulbs are usually restricted to deciduous forests and typically produce their leaves and flowers only when the highest levels of rain and sunlight reach the forest floor. This is during late autumn, winter, and early spring, when the surrounding trees are leafless. In the summer months, when the dense canopy of tree leaves prevents much rain or sunlight from reaching the ground, woodland bulbs survive underground.

Cut a daffodil bulb down the center and you will find fully developed flower and leaf buds that are ready to emerge from the ground as soon as spring arrives.

Buyer Beware: A Gardener's Guide to Bulb Conservation

Plants sold at your local garden center and through catalogs usually originate somewhere else many miles away. If you don't already, it's a good idea to inquire where the bulbs you are interested in buying come from, and to make sure that purchasing them will not contribute to the species' demise.

Each year, millions of bulbs sold in North America are dug up from wild places in Turkey, southeastern Europe, Hungary, and the Republic of Georgia, depleting native bulb populations and driving some species closer to extinction. In the year 2000 alone, 1,600,000 bulbs of three species, *Galanthus elwesii* (giant snowdrop), *Sternbergia lutea* (winter or fall daffodil), and *Cyclamen hederifolium* (hardy cyclamen) were imported into the United States, according to the World Wildlife Fund, which through its TRAFFIC program tracks international trade in species considered to be threatened or endangered. As many as two thirds of these bulbs were collected in the wild; most of them were giant snowdrops. Other bulbs sometimes collected in the wild include additional species of snowdrops and sternbergias and, less often, winter aconite (*Eranthis hyemalis*) and anemones (*Anemone*).

Bulbs are collected in the wild for several reasons: They are easy to dig and transport over long distances during their dormant period. Many are native to economically depressed areas where people supplement their meager incomes through bulb collection. And of course, there is the strong demand for bulbs by gardeners around the globe.

The Netherlands is the hub of the flower-bulb industry, and most of the wild-collected bulbs from Turkey move through Holland on their way to gardens in other European countries and the United States. In an attempt to reduce the number of wild-collected bulbs, Dutch bulb purveyors now label wild bulbs marketed from Holland as "Bulbs from wild source" or "Bulbs from wild stock." The trade in many bulb species is controlled under an international agreement called the Convention on International Trade in Endangered Species of Wild Fauna and Flora (CITES). More than 150 countries, including the United States and Canada, participate in the agreement. In another encouraging initiative, international non-profit organizations and governments are cooperating in efforts to encourage Turkish farmers to cultivate bulbs sustainably rather than collect them from the wild. In fact, the Turkish government establishes and enforces an annual wild harvest quota for several bulb species in an effort to keep exploitation within levels that do not endanger wild populations.

Easy to dig and transport when dormant, bulbs are frequently taken from the wild and sold commercially. If done irresponsibly, the practice may endanger native bulb populations. Above are giant snowdrop, *Galanthus elwesii,* **and winter aconite,** *Eranthis hyemalis.*

Nevertheless, national and international laws and agreements may be difficult to enforce, so gardeners have an important role to play in reducing the trade in wild-collected bulbs. If possible, select cultivars (cultivated varieties, the plants with names in single quotes after their Latin names), because these are propagated in nurseries, not dug from the wild. When you do purchase species bulbs (the ones with only the Latin names and no additional cultivar name in single quotes), ask where they are from, and buy only those that are propagated or harvested from the wild under a quota system that can be verified. Ask for the name of the propagator. But keep in mind that not all wild collection of bulbs is bad. In fact, purchasing responsibly harvested bulbs can help communities use these resources in a sustainable manner. Turkey's quota system for plants is actually among the best in the world and has been praised for its sound management. Keep your eye out for nurseries and other sources promoting such sustainably collected bulbs. If we all express interest in these plants, they will increasingly become commercially available.

—*Beth Hanson*

A STEP-BY-STEP GUIDE:
Growing Bulbs Successfully

KATIE STANNARD

Gardeners are the most optimistic people on the planet. We dig holes in the ground, drop bulbs in, and wait—sometimes as long as six months—and may even forget along the way what we planted and where. But when the first cheery blooms of snowdrops (*Galanthus*), winter aconite (*Eranthis hyemalis*), or crocus begin to light up our gardens, we know we were right all along to be hopeful.

Great bulb gardeners are not only optimistic but also curious and adventurous. They balance their enthusiasm and experimental spirit with solid information about the cultural needs of different bulbs—the what, where, how, and when of bulb planting. Keep in mind that bulbs are easy to grow. They come with everything they need to bloom the very first year already packed inside them.

Selecting Bulbs

Choosing the bulbs that will grow best in your garden is easier when you are familiar with the likes and dislikes of different bulbs and consider how well you'll be able to accommodate their needs. Here are some tips to help you choose the right bulbs for your garden.

Do your homework. Find out which bulbs grow well in your area. Check with local experts, such as your county extension office, who often can recommend bulbs and other plants well suited to the area. Other great resources include gardening groups, plant societies, good garden centers or nurseries, and neighbors.

Know your zone. Selecting bulbs that are well suited to your climate is critical. If you don't know it already, find out your hardiness zone (for a map of the

To succeed with bulbs, select varieties that are suited to the growing conditions in your yard. Most fritillaries, for example, prefer very well drained soil. Opposite is *Fritillaria imperialis* 'Lutea Maxima'.

Tulips, such as 'Philippe de Comines', at left, prefer rather dry soil conditions in summer. Unlike most fritillaries, snake's-head fritillary, *Fritillaria meleagris*, at right, prefers to stay moist during summer dormancy.

USDA hardiness zones, see page 101), and make sure the bulbs you want to grow are hardy in your area. Books and good mail-order catalogs note specific zone recommendations for different bulbs, and most bulb packages you buy in garden centers will provide the same information. Bear in mind that vendors can be overly optimistic about zone recommendations, but this will encourage you to experiment by pushing the zone limits of various plants.

Know the growing conditions in your garden. Proper soil moisture is vital for bulb health. The most important piece of information I can share is this: Most bulbs do best in loose, fertile, well-drained soil. Most spring-blooming bulbs also prefer soil that stays pretty dry during the summer when they are dormant. The number-one cause of early bulb decline is soil that stays too damp for too long, which may be due to poor drainage, too much moisture, or a combination of both. Bulbs are often planted in beds with moisture-loving annuals and perennials. But tulips and hyacinths, native to dry-summer central Asia, do not take kindly to the frequent summer waterings these other plants require. If tulips and hyacinths don't return and rebloom year after year, too much summer moisture may be to blame.

Then again, there are some bulbs that require regular moisture in the summer. Snowdrops, winter aconite, snake's-head fritillary (*Fritillaria meleagris*), and camassias prefer humus-rich, well-drained soil that never goes bone-dry in the summer. Generally, these bulbs are smaller or fleshier and need the summer moisture to ensure good growth and basic survival. These are the bulbs to plant with your moisture-loving perennials.

As you peruse catalogs or garden-center selections, it's important to determine whether the bulbs you like will actually perform well in your garden's growing conditions, or if you need to set aside time for the important work of improving the soil and drainage.

Know where the sun shines in your garden. Most bulbs do best year after year when planted in full sun. Daffodils (*Narcissus*), snowflakes (*Leucojum*), and small early-blooming bulbs like crocuses and Siberian squill (*Scilla siberica*) tolerate some shade. In the South these bulbs actually seem to prefer it, especially when they are planted under deciduous trees that leaf out after the bulbs have completed much of their growth cycle. Snowdrops, snake's-head fritillaries, and winter aconite prefer light shade, where the soil is somewhat cooler. Consult the cultural instructions that accompany your bulbs for specifics on which bulbs need warm or cool soil, full sun, or light shade in your area.

Know what a healthy bulb looks like. When making bulb selections it helps to know what is considered "normal" for a particular type of bulb in terms of size, shape, and firmness. Size is a complicated issue. Most online or mail-order catalogs list the approximate sizes of their bulbs, such as "15 to 17 cm," which is the circumference measured in centimeters. Comparing prices and sizes is important because what looks like a bargain may get you smaller, immature bulbs. To further muddy the waters, species or antique varieties often are genetically smaller than modern hybrids, both in bulb and overall plant size. For example, compare the gorgeous red and white species tulip *Tulipa clusiana* or lady tulip with the modern Darwin tulip 'Golden Apeldoorn'. The bulb of the former is the size of a macadamia nut, and the plant grows to 21 inches, while the latter bulb is the size of a plum and grows to 24 inches. Many gardeners are discovering that heirloom and species bulbs add an important dimension of tradition and wildflowerlike grace to their gardens.

That being said, within a specific variety, bigger is better: A larger bulb will likely produce more or taller foliage and more robust blooms. Just be sure to check sizes listed in various catalogs, and look for language such as "all of our bulbs are blooming size."

When you buy bulbs, pick firm and solid ones, unless you're purchasing naturally fleshy bulbs, such as fritillaries, Spanish bluebells (*Hyacinthoides hispanica*), or camassias. Small blemishes or bits of mold generally won't affect bulb performance, though it's wise to make sure there's not a larger soft or rotting spot underneath a patch of mold.

Know what to expect when picking out bulbs: Choose firm and solid specimens, except when buying naturally fleshy bulbs such as fritillary, shown at left, or Spanish bluebells and camassias.

Preparing the Soil

Since good drainage and the right moisture level are critical for bulb health, what should you do if you don't have that ideal friable, humus-rich, well-drained soil? The task of turning a sand or clay bed into bulb paradise may be a bit daunting, but the long-term benefits for bulbs and other plants will be well worth the effort.

As most bulbs should be planted no deeper than about 8 inches, you should loosen and amend the soil to a depth of 12 inches. If you are working in clay soil, adding compost and chunky organic matter while turning over the bed will greatly aid in loosening the soil. A great way to improve drainage in clay soils is to create raised beds on top of the existing soil, using good organic amendments and keeping in mind that a 12-inch-deep bed is better for bulb health than a 4-inch-deep bed.

Happily for those of us with unrelenting clay, there are several bulb varieties that actually thrive in clay soils and soggy spots, including the larger snowflakes, campernelle daffodils (*Narcissus × odorus*) and the tazetta daffodil 'Grand Primo'.

If your soil is quite sandy, add compost, coir, or other water-holding organic materials. Compost also provides nutrients to the soil, encourages beneficial insects and bacteria, and discourages harmful pests. Check with local resources such as your county extension office for more specific advice on addressing your particular soil needs. In order to determine precisely what your soil requires, have your soil tested through your county extension service. For a nominal fee, the soil will be analyzed for nutrient content, and based on the soil and nutrient requirements of the plants you want to grow, the extension service will make suggestions for soil amendments.

For the rare occasion when the number of bulbs purchased and hours available for preparing the bed and planting exceed the reality of the time-space continuum, here's a tip for planting quickly in soil that's not suited to your bulbs' needs. Buy a large bag of compost to use as your ready-made "amended" soil, and dig a wide hole or a trench to accommodate your bulbs. Space the bulbs a little closer than recommended, setting tulips, daffodils, and hyacinths near the bottom of the hole, filling in with a layer of compost, and planting smaller bulbs in successive layers. Use the remaining compost to fill the hole, water well, and mulch with leaves, straw, or pine needles. Then vow to do better next year!

When to Plant

If you've ever been to a garden center in August, I bet you've seen the signs proclaiming Now Is the Time to Plant Bulbs. The public might be better served if they instead said Buy Now, Plant Later. Generally, you can plant most spring-blooming bulbs in the fall when soil temperatures in your area drop to about 60° F.

Don't panic if there's an early-season frost or frosts. The ground stays warmer much longer than the surrounding air, so you should still have plenty of time for planting. In my Zone 5b garden, I've planted tulips at Thanksgiving and, snow permitting, into December as well, and I've heard tales of other Michigan gardeners who plant tulips in January!

In most zones, small bulbs should be planted as soon as the soil is cool enough. They dry out more easily in storage than larger bulbs, and as they are planted more shallowly, they are subject to freezing earlier. What's more, if planted early, they have enough time to develop good root systems before the ground freezes. This group of "small bulbs" includes crocuses, snowdrops (*Galanthus*), and grape hyacinths (*Muscari*). Any of the fleshy bulbs that prefer more moisture should also be planted earlier, including fritillaries, Spanish bluebells, and camassias. Next, plant hyacinths and daffodils, which root better if the soil is not too cool, and finally tulips, which prefer the coolest soil.

Planting Techniques

The "three times" rule is a good rule of thumb to use when planting spring bulbs: Plant the bulbs at a depth three times the height of the bulb, and space them three

times their width apart. Plant 2-inch bulbs 6 inches deep—that is, 6 inches from the soil level to the bottom of the planting hole. Plant with the pointy side of the bulb facing up. If you can't tell which is the rooting side and which is the sprouting side, plant the bulb on its side. It will figure out which way is up! Other basic guidelines: Plant larger bulbs deeper, smaller bulbs less so. Plant deeper in

Most bulbs do best when planted in full sun, but some, such as summer snowflake, *Leucojum aestivum*, tolerate some shade.

Small bulbs, such as grape hyacinth, *Muscari armeniacum,* shown here with yellow and purple pansies, are prone to dry out quickly in storage and should be planted as soon as the soil cools off in early fall.

sandy soils, less so in heavy soils. Plant deeper in the North, less so in the South. Planting deeper helps protect the bulbs against cold and is also said to help enhance the longevity of bulbs and keep them from dividing into so many smaller bulbs that blooming suffers.

Plant larger bulbs, such as full-size tulips, hyacinths, and daffodils, at a depth of about 8 inches, and install smaller-size daffodils, such as 'W.P. Milner' or jonquils *(Narcissus jonquilla)*, 5 to 6 inches deep. Plant crocuses and snowdrops 2 to 3 inches deep.

The "three times" rule should help to produce a nicely spaced look; plant closer together for a lusher look. Spacing bulbs farther apart—6 to 8 inches for larger bulbs and 4 to 5 inches for smaller ones—will give them a bit more room to increase over the long run, which is especially important in a naturalized setting. Again, be sure to consult the cultural instructions for your bulbs.

One other handy tip for planting: Carry a ruler with your planting tools or a trowel with measurements marked on the handle or shaft in permanent pen. This is a fast and easy way to check proper depth and spacing for new bulbs.

Watering and Fertilizing

Most bulbs do better with regular fertilizing, and bulb fertilizer is one good choice. Some gardeners prefer to use bone meal (though the way it is processed today saps most of its nutrients) or rock phosphate. Even better is a healthy dose of compost—in fact, if you regularly improve the overall quality of your soil with compost and other organic amendments, you won't have to provide much fertilizer for most bulbs. Mix compost or fertilizer into the soil when you're planting or top-dress, following label directions. To help boost the bulbs for next year's bloom you can also top-dress the soil in the spring after blooming. Remember to work any fertilizers well into the soil, and avoid high-nitrogen fertilizers (like lawn fertilizer).

Water the soil well after you've planted your bulbs, and maintain good soil moisture from fall through spring (when the soil isn't frozen) to help with good rooting and bulb growth. If the winter is especially dry and mild, you may want to check periodically to make sure that the soil is moist enough.

Spring and Summer Bulb Care

It's essential that you let all bulb foliage and stems mature and fade to yellow before you remove them, as the nutrients they store during this period feed the bulbs for next spring's flowering. Wait at least six weeks after blooming before you cut or mow. As soon as the foliage yellows you can remove it, then cover any holes left in the ground from the flower stalks lightly with soil to keep pests out. Feel free to cut off spent flower heads to

SIX TIPS FOR SPECTACULAR BULB DISPLAYS

1. Plant bulbs in areas where you can see them in bloom from a window inside your house.

2. Plant an entire bed with bulbs from each major bulb type for a full season of blooms—clumps of crocuses, a swath of hyacinths, multiple groupings of daffodils and tulips. You'll be amazed at the changing range of colors over the many weeks of spring.

3. Think about where you could use a little color or something bright in your yard. Plant an easy patch of crocuses, daffodils, or squills under deciduous trees, by the front steps, or around the base of an unsightly utility pole.

4. Plant plenty of early-season bulbs like crocuses and snowdrops. They take up very little room, and you'll never regret starting the growing season earlier.

5. Plant a ribbon of six or more varieties of hyacinths for a fabulous display of old-fashioned beauty, fragrance, and color (ranging from magenta and purple-black to apricot, pink, primrose, sand, and sky-blue). Heirloom hyacinths are also the most endangered of all garden bulbs, so planting them helps to preserve a vanishing horticultural heritage.

6. Intersperse bulbs with native plants well suited to your garden. Many native plants need little or no supplemental water over the summer, making them ideal companion plants for tulips, hyacinths, or daffodils.

prevent seed formation, except for those bulbs you want to self-sow, such as *Crocus tommasinianus*, snowdrops, winter aconite, grape hyacinths, and squills. Then ensure that the bulbs stay as dry as possible during the summer months, except for those noted above. If you want to provide the driest possible summer conditions, consider the age-old technique of lifting out tulips or hyacinths after the foliage has yellowed and storing them dry in a cool basement or storage area over the summer. Then simply replant the bulbs again in the fall and fertilize. Using bulb-planting baskets will help you to locate these bulbs when it's time to dig them up.

You may also want to consider planting companions that will help camouflage aging bulb foliage, combining self-seeding, old-fashioned annuals like nicotianas, larkspurs (*Consolida*), johnny jump-ups (*Viola tricolor*), corn poppies (*Papaver rhoeas*), or forget-me-nots (*Myosotis*) with early-summer perennials, native plants, or hostas. Also, planting bulbs in narrow, foot-wide drifts or swaths helps make the maturing foliage seem to disappear among the other growing plants, a marvelous recommendation from Gertrude Jekyll.

With just a little effort, bulbs will provide much enjoyment in your garden. In today's rush-rush world, bulb planting—which makes us slow down and wait through the cold and rain and snow of winter—is one of gardening's greatest gifts of optimism and hope.

DETERRING DEER AND OTHER PESTS

If you want to feed the deer, rabbits, squirrels, and woodchucks in your neighborhood, keep in mind that they prefer a diet rich in tulips! If you'd like to see your bulbs actually bloom in spring, select from the many other gorgeous bulbs that are more animal-resistant, including daffodils, hyacinths, *Crocus tommasinianus*, Spanish bluebells, fritillaries, grape hyacinths, snowdrops, squills, and alliums.

If animals try to dig your newly planted bulbs, cover the beds with plastic bird netting, hardware cloth, or old window screens for a couple of weeks until the inviting smell of freshly dug earth has dissipated. If animals burrow to your bulbs, try exclusionary tactics such as lining the planting hole with hardware cloth, or plant in hardware-cloth boxes, buried pots, or plastic planting baskets covered with a square of chicken wire.

If animals like to dig your freshly planted bulbs, try covering the beds.

You can treat tulips with bitter, nontoxic Ro-pel spray before planting, and if you find that animals eat spring growth, spraying at that time with Ro-pel will help immensely too. Other tactics to discourage animal buffets include covering spring growth with chicken wire, erecting a low chicken-wire fence, or sprinkling blood meal around the bulb bed.

Daffodils are the most critter-resistant bulbs, so you may be thrilled to discover, as I did, that there is an astonishing diversity of daffodils—way beyond yellow trumpets—including many fragrant varieties. I confess a personal fondness for double daffodils, with their explosion of sometimes frothy and frilled petals, such as 'Irene Copeland', 'Rip van Winkle', and 'Double Campernelle'. Daffodils also come in varied colors and shapes, like the soft apricot-and-cream trumpet 'Mrs. R.O. Backhouse', the shocking tangerine and white 'Dick Wellband', the ball-gown-shaped 'Hoop Petticoats', and the sweet-as-spring tiny-cup jonquil 'Early Louisiana'. If you think you've seen it all in daffodils, these heirloom varieties will provide wonderful surprises in your garden. Best of all, daffodils stand the best chance of lasting year after year; not only are they animal-resistant but they tolerate summer moisture better than most bulbs.

ORCHESTRATING A RIOT OF BLOOM:

A Spring-Bulb Design Primer

C. COLSTON BURRELL

he sheer exuberance of spring-flowering bulbs is a delight to our winter-weary, color-starved eyes. Their flowers burst forth from late January to June in a full range of hues—blue, purple, pink, red, orange, yellow, white, and green. In my own garden in Virginia, I anticipate the earliest bulbs with the same impatience that I await the return of the robins and the catkins on the willows. Just after the winter solstice, I search for the first green noses of the plants that will soon flaunt their flowers in the face of winter's chill breezes. In mid-January clumps of white snowdrops (*Galanthus*) pop out of the ground, usually beating out the crocuses and cyclamens by a week or two. By mid-February, the first daffodils (*Narcissus*) add their cheery yellow to the awakening garden. When spring finally arrives, early daffodils are past their prime, but anemones, species tulips, starflowers (*Ipheion*), late daffodils, and Spanish bluebells (*Hyacinthoides hispanica*), as well as native bulbs like trout lilies (*Erythronium americanum*) and jack-in-the-pulpits (*Arisaema*), rise to take their place. In early May tulips steal the show. As spring wanes, there are still plenty of bulbs to come. Late tulips, camassias, ornamental onions (*Allium*), Dutch iris hybrids, and foxtail lilies (*Eremurus*) carry the garden into early summer.

Spring bulbs have been garden mainstays since colonial times. The clipped box parterre gardens of colonial Williamsburg, Virginia, featured bulbs to add color and fragrance to the spring season, as did early cottage dooryards in New England. The most exhilarating bulb planting I have ever seen is the display along the lime walk in the gardens of Sissinghurst Castle in Kent, England. In April, this garden is in full glory with thousands of different bulbs blooming in unison. Sweeps of tulips, hyacinths, and late daffodils emerge among clumps of

Masses of tiny spring starflower, *Ipheion uniflorum*, surround tulips and anemones.

Paint a colorful picture by combining bulbs with perennials and shrubs that bloom at the same time. Above, the lilac creates a backdrop for tulips 'China Pink' and 'Red Pomponette', grown through a carpet of red-flowering English daisy, *Bellis perennis*.

trout lilies, fritillaries, and grape hyacinths (*Muscari*), all above a tightly woven carpet of starflowers, fume root (*Corydalis*), and anemones in shades of blue, pink, and white. The garden is so chock-full of bulbs, you couldn't squeeze in another one with a shoehorn. Though most of us cannot duplicate such splendor, we can make a statement if we plant even a dozen bulbs.

Context and Contrast

Too often flowering bulbs are lined up in front of a wall or hedge in single file, as if they were doomed rebels facing a firing squad. Instead of ostracizing your bulbs, let them mingle with perennials, ferns, grasses, and shrubs. The synergistic effect will knock your socks off, something a lonely cluster of red and yellow tulips left to bloom and fade alone at the base of a mailbox or lamppost will never achieve. Attractive when viewed against a backdrop of complementary foliage and flowers, bulbs fit into every garden situation, from containers and formal bedding schemes to mixed borders, rock gardens, meadows, and rambling woodland walks.

Place drifts or scattered clusters between clumps of perennials or use bulbs to skirt the bases of shrubs. The foliage of emerging perennials such as phlox, daylilies (*Hemerocallis*), peonies (*Paeonia*), and catmints (*Nepeta*) will hide the declining leaves of daffodils and tulips that otherwise look tatty until early summer. At the front of a bed it's best to use dwarf bulbs, such as European wood anemone (*Anemone nemorosa*) or striped squill (*Puschkinia scilloides*) as well as species forms of tulips and daffodils, which grow into much smaller plants than their hybrid cousins. All have small leaves that die away discreetly, so there's no untidy foliage to detract from the garden. Clustering at least a dozen of one kind is usually preferable to dotting bulbs throughout a bed haphazardly.

Pair the spiky, finely textured foliage common to most bulbs with medium and boldly textured plants as well as prostrate and rounded forms. Some classic plant pairings include snowdrops (*Galanthus*) dotted among clumps of hellebores, Virginia bluebell *(Mertensia virginica)* with white daffodils, and pale yellow tulips with creamy primroses (*Primula*). The flowers of some bulbs like trumpet daffodils and fritillaries are large, even though the foliage is fine, so you may need both small- and large-leafed plants for balance. Taller daffodils and tulips seem to float above medium-textured leaves. Contrast the finely textured but bold heads of ornamental onions with large, bold flowers such as peonies. Set off by groundcovers, sedges, grasses, emerging perennials, ferns, and shrubs, your bulbs will look beautiful. And once the spring bloomers vanish below ground in early summer, herbaceous plants and shrubs become the focus of the garden.

Color Matters

Though an informal pastiche of color is delightful in the early-spring garden, by carefully considering bulb bloom times and flower colors you can create subtle harmony or dramatic contrast and enhance the overall color scheme of your garden. If you want a jolt of color to jumpstart spring, plant bulbs that emerge very early. Snowdrops are among the first bulb flowers to open, anytime between late January and April, depending on where you live. If you place them with dark-flowered hellebores that open at about the same time you will accentuate the contrast between the two colors. Use yellow winter aconite (*Eranthis hyemalis*) under early-flowering butter-yellow or orange witch-hazel *(Hamamelis)* or primrose-yellow winter hazel *(Corylopsis pauciflora)* for a bright color harmony. A carpet of glory-of-the-snow (*Chionodoxa*), anemones, and trout lilies looks lovely blanketing the ground among the awakening crowns of clumping ferns like *Dryopteris* and *Polystichum*. As the season progresses, the expanding fronds will obscure the ripening bulb foliage.

Bold Bulbs

Hybrid tulips have the reputation of being short-lived, so many gardeners pass them over for the more predictable results of daffodils and crocuses. Why not enjoy hybrid tulips, knowing they will not perennialize? I treat them as annuals in shaded spots and reap all of the joy with none of the disappointment. Use a dozen tulips to add height and lift to a less-than-spectacular-looking corner of the

Pink lily-flowered tulip 'Jacqueline' and sweet broom, *Genista* × *spachiana*, add a splash of bright color.

garden and it comes alive. Spruce up a quiet, shaded area with a drift of tulips in contrasting or harmonious colors, depending on your taste. Tulip bulbs are inexpensive, and the reward is great for little effort. If they are not meant to be permanent, you can cut the yellowing foliage to the ground or pull the plants out after flowering. Try double white 'Mt. Tacoma' with white bleeding hearts *(Dicentra spectabilis* 'Alba') and blue phlox *(Phlox divaricata)*, or pink 'Angélique' with rosy *Dicentra spectabilis* and white barrenwort *(Epimedium* × *youngianum* 'Niveum'). Pastel color combinations are easy. Combine soft pink tulips with white narcissus and soft blue 'Valerie Finnis' grape hyacinth. Pale blue *Ipheion* is lovely with white and soft yellow bicolor 'Lemon Drop' daffodils and creamy 'Yellow Present' tulips. For late spring, orange 'Generaal de Wet' tulips bloom amongst the sepia blades of leatherleaf sedge *(Carex buchananii)*. I use this floral wealth to create exciting combinations that temporarily take center stage like actors vying for a part in a one-act play.

Daffodils excel in any garden setting. I planted 'Jetfire', a bicolor with a yellow perianth (sepals and petals) and an orange cup, behind clumps of deep cherry-red primroses with deep orange centers *(Primula* 'Avondale'), and the combination is fantastic in front of soft orange *Chaenomeles* × *superba* 'Cameo' and intense red *Hamamelis* 'Diana'. The witch-hazel blooms in late winter above a carpet of winter aconite, both of which fade as the daffodils open.

For dramatic effect, plant tangerine-colored crown imperial *(Fritillaria imperialis* 'Primeur') with burgundy-leafed *Euphorbia amygdaloides* 'Rubra', 'Orange Emperor' tulips, and billowing clumps of bronze *Carex buchanani*. Orange and purple bicolored wallflowers *(Erysimum)* look great with early tulip 'Purple Prince' and deep golden or orange daffodils like 'Pappy George'. Try chartreuse *Fritillaria pallidiflora* with variegated Hakone grass *(Hakonechloa macra* 'Aureola'), purple hellebores, and blue-flowered squill *(Scilla bifolia)*, or deep blue grape hyacinth with rose and yellow 'Elegant Lady' tulips and a pink-cup daffodil such as 'Katy Heath'.

Subtle Schemes

Many species bulbs and some miniature or dwarf hybrids are small-flowered, so they have more visual impact when planted in large clumps or bold sweeps. Carpets of winter aconite and English bluebells under the towering tulip poplars at Winterthur Museum and Gardens in Delaware have inspired generations of gardeners to grow spring-flowering bulbs. Sheets of snowdrops, *Crocus tommasinianus,* and grape hyacinths seen self-sowing freely around old homesteads give hope to gardeners who plant bulbs a dozen at a time and wait for them to spread.

Bulbs with short stature, such as spring snowflake (*Leucojum vernum*), scillas, and golden star (*Triteleia ixioides* 'Starlite') look best erupting through a low groundcover with small leaves such as sweet woodruff (*Galium odoratum*) or creeping phlox (*Phlox stolonifera*); these will not overwhelm the bulbs' flowers.

In a rock garden, plant a succession of dwarf bulbs, such as species daffodils and tulips, dwarf ornamental onions, oxalis, and rue anemone (*Anemonella thalictroides*) to add color among dwarf shrubs and conifers. Delicate bulbs like *Brimeura, Ixiolirion,* and Ithuriel's spear (*Triteleia laxa*) often show to best advantage in a rock garden, free of the lush foliage and large flowers of traditional garden plants that may overwhelm or outshine them. Basket-of-gold (*Aurinia saxatalis*), aubretia

Top: Before the crape myrtle leafs out, sweeps of spring starflower, Ipheion uniflorum, attract all the attention.

Bottom: Adding color but needing little care, spring bulbs, such as these daffodils, liven up grassy areas.

(*Aubrieta*), wild buckwheat (*Eriogonum*), and primroses (*Primula*) are colorful spring-blooming companions for small bulbs. Pinks (*Dianthus*), beard-tongues (*Penstemon*), saxifrages, sedums (*Hylotelephium*), thyme, and other spreading plants will fill the void left by yellowing foliage.

Some unusual bulbs, such as *Calochortus,* many *Fritillaria* species, and Chilean blue crocus (*Tecophilaea cyanocrocus*) demand rock-garden conditions to succeed outside their native grassland or desert habitats. Plant them in clumps or drifts so their delicate flowers will show up from a distance, and surround them with dwarf grasses, alpine ferns, *Lewisia*, cacti, and other showy dryland plants. If you do not have room or desire for a rock garden, try these delicate bulbs in a trough garden placed on a deck or patio.

Bulbs can even spill over into the less manicured areas of the garden where they add color with little care. Naturalize daffodils, crocuses, snowdrops, and myriad others in the rough grass of an orchard or meadow, or even in your lawn. Choose strong-growing hybrids listed in catalogs for naturalizing, or better yet, species that will reproduce by offsets and by self-sown seed. If you plant bulbs in your lawn, mow the grass close in late winter, before the tender shoots emerge, then take a break until the bulb foliage is fully ripened. If you naturalize only dwarf bulbs, not overblown daffodils or tall tulips, you can set the mower blade high and cut right above the growing leaves without damaging them.

In this California garden, annual chrysanthemums will hide the declining tulip foliage later in the season. In colder regions, perennials can camouflage dying bulb leaves.

Left: Hellebores, bluebells, and daffodils add subtle hues to a woodland walk in spring. Right: Blue phlox and North American native jack-in-the-pulpit, *Arisaema triphyllum*, make a striking pair.

In a woodland setting, wild species and smaller selections blend in better than gaudy hybrids. Their delicate flowers are more in keeping with native woodland wildflowers and ferns. Most deciduous shrubs allow ample light through their branches in spring, allowing bulbs to bloom freely. Plan combinations around early-flowering shrubs such as wintersweet (*Chimonanthus praecox*), jasmine (*Jasminum nudiflorum*), forsythia, and fragrant viburnum (*Viburnum carlesii*). Snowdrops, glory-of-the-snow, winter aconite, and cyclamen will greet the first warm days together with the flowers of the shrubs. Pale, primrose-yellow winter hazel underplanted with soft yellow daffodils and blue-flowering squill (*Scilla bifolia*) is enchanting. White-flowering quince (*Chaenomeles speciosa*) sets off blue glory-of-the-snow, daffodils, anemones, and early Kaufman tulips.

The beauty of spring-blooming bulbs lies in their early flowering and ephemeral nature. Save for a few long-lasting daffodils, most are as fleeting as spring green itself. To celebrate this tenuous place in the spring sun, devise combinations that show your bulbs to best effect when they look their best, and hide them in their inevitable decline. Attention to detail and judicious placement will get your garden off to a colorful start. Whether you plant a carefully orchestrated border scheme, a bluebell dell, or a single container of tulips on your balcony, bulbs enliven spring and fill the air with enticing fragrance.

BRIMMING WITH BULBS:

Container Gardens That Capture the Essence of Spring

MARK FISHER

fter a cold, dark winter, we all long for a sign of spring—even something as subtle as a crocus bloom peeking through the snow or the delicious smell of a hyacinth on a bright, cool spring morning. You can capture a little bit of that spring feeling by filling containers, whether barrels, buckets, boxes, pots, jars, or troughs, with spring-flowering bulbs. Pots of spring bulbs expand your garden space and allow you to extend the bloom season in a protected spot on the patio or terrace.

Container Choices

The first step is finding suitable containers. The styles and sizes you choose will form the framework of your design and determine whether your bulb display has a formal, informal, or eclectic feel. I prefer containers made of fiberglass, heavy plastic, or wood to those made of clay, which tend to crack easily if exposed to alternating freezing and thawing during the winter.

No matter what style or material strikes your fancy, be sure to pick pots that are at least 16 inches across and 12 inches deep. The containers need to be large enough to give the bulbs room to develop strong root systems, which will keep them from being forced up and out of the soil as it freezes in winter. The larger the container, the longer the soil will stay moist, and it may not even freeze solid during the coldest days of the year. Adequate drainage holes are another important consideration. A container that's 18 or so inches across should have at least three holes about half an inch wide. Larger containers, 24 inches or more across, often have one 1-inch hole, usually in the center of the base.

A strawberry jar planted for spring: The flowers of *Tulipa tarda* rise above the top, while the foliage of spent crocuses peeks from the pockets.

Potting Soils

Once you've assembled the containers, it's time to consider the planting medium. Bulbs generally require soil that drains well and retains moisture; they are prone to rot in soggy or heavy soil. The ideal container mix absorbs water quickly and holds its shape when you take a handful and squeeze it.

You can make your own planting medium by mixing compost with sand in a ratio of 2 to 1, or you can use a commercial mix. As most of these are peat-based, they have a tendency to hold a lot of water, so it's usually a good idea to amend them with a little coarse sand to promote drainage. Avoid potting mixes that contain a lot of perlite. Over time the white pellets tend to float to the top of the container, where they look a little out of place.

Bulb Combinations

When it comes to choosing plant combinations for containers, you have tremendous latitude. You can base your design on combinations of colors, bulb varieties and heights, bloom times, and fragrance.

Color sets the mood of your design. Tulip combinations such as purple and orange or red and yellow are brilliant and eye-popping. You can use dark-flowered tulips with taller varieties in lighter shades for a nice effect. Monochromatic

schemes using different bulb varieties can create an interesting effect, or you can go for high contrast by mixing white flowers with very dark ones. For a whimsical touch, mix tall, dark maroon varieties with shorter yellow varieties. Plant individual containers with one variety, or mix different bulbs in one pot and group them together.

Choose plants with different blooming heights to give accent and dimension to your composition. One common approach is to plant tall flower

Increase your gardening space and bring some color to your front door by taking the time in fall to plant pots with some of your favorite spring bulbs.

varieties toward the center of the container and surround them with shorter plants. If you have a pot that's at least 30 inches across, try planting three groups of taller varieties using five to seven bulbs per group. For example, mix different classes of tulips, such as doubles and single- or lily-flowering varieties. A short pink double tulip planted with a mix of pink lily-flowered tulips and pink Darwin hybrids makes an appealing combination.

You can lengthen the bloom season by combining bulb species with different flowering times, all in one pot if you like. As one variety fades, another starts to bloom. This approach requires you to imagine how your composition will unfold over time. Remember that as the blooms of the earlier varieties fade, they will leave their foliage behind. It's a nice idea to soften the coarse foliage of tulips by mixing them with crocuses, which have attractive, grasslike leaves.

Develop a focal point for each container that changes as the season progresses, otherwise you may end up with a "hole" in your design. With careful planning you can create several different combinations that will keep your pot flowering for two to three months. Start your container blooming with early-flowering species cro-cuses such as *Crocus chrysanthus, C. ancyrensis,* and *C tommasinianus.* As these fade, early varieties of fragrant narcissus or tulips start to open, then wonderfully fragrant hyacinths, followed by later varieties of narcissus and tulips, which will bloom into late May.

Planting the Containers

Once you've determined how you want to combine plants, you are ready to start potting. Spring-flowering bulbs need to be planted in the fall when cool soil temperatures —about 40°F—will prompt rooting, which takes four to six weeks. This means that if you live in the Northeast, for example, you should plant bulbs in pots in early October, about when you remove summer annuals from containers. Most bulbs also require a cold period of about 12 to 16 weeks to get properly estab-lished (the length of the cold period varies, depending on the species).

Plant larger bulbs first. Fill the soil level in the container to the correct plant-ing depth for the large bulbs. If you start with tulips, for example, fill a container that's 12 inches deep with 6 inches of soil. Place the bulbs on top of the soil and cover them with about 3 inches of soil. Then plant the smaller bulbs at this level and cover with additional soil.

The rule of thumb is to plant bulbs at a depth three times the diameter of the bulb. In other words, plant tulips, narcissus, and hyacinths about 4 to 6 inches deep meas-ured from the base of the bulb and smaller bulbs such as crocuses, anemones, and glory-of-the-snow (*Chionodoxa*) 2 to 3 inches deep. For a lush look, set the smaller bulbs close together, just 2 to 3 inches apart. Space larger bulbs 6 inches apart.

When planting tulips, you will notice that one side of the bulb is flattish and the other side more rounded. If you are planting tulips around the edges of a

No matter what style or material you pick, be sure to choose a pot that's at least 16 inches across and 12 inches deep, so the bulbs have enough room to develop strong root systems. The barrel above is planted with daffodils, tulips, and grape hyacinths.

container, turn the bulbs so their flat sides face the wall. As the tulips emerge in spring, the first leaf will unfurl toward the flat portion of the bulb and over the edge of the pot, softening it. With other bulbs, just be sure to plant them with the pointed end facing up. Once you've planted all the bulbs, water them thoroughly. Depending on the size of your pot, you may have to water weekly to keep the soil evenly moist.

When winter arrives, mulch the containers with a 3-inch layer of leaves, shredded bark or coco, or evergreen boughs left over from the holidays (you can pile the branches about 5 inches thick). Mulching will reduce the effects of repeated freezing and thawing, which commonly occurs in early spring and may push the bulbs out of the soil.

Check the container periodically throughout the winter to be sure that the soil is moist—and so that you can witness the emergence of the bulb buds. Start removing most of the mulch when the plants are about an inch tall. Leave a 1-inch layer of bark or coco mulch on the soil to give the container a finished look.

By the time the last of the spring-flowering bulbs fade, the warmer weather will have arrived, and you can start planting your containers with summer flowers. 🌷🌷🌷

ANYTHING-BUT-DUSTY ANTIQUES:
Heirloom Bulbs for Every Garden

SCOTT KUNST

eirloom bulbs are not dusty has-beens, as more and more gardeners are discovering with delight. Most are gorgeous, many are unusual, and they often out-perform modern cultivars. What's more, all can bring to your garden a rich, living connection to the past.

Heirloom bulbs go by many names: antique bulbs, heritage bulbs, historic, vintage, classic, legacy, and old-fashioned bulbs. Some people try to define them by date—for example, bulbs that were introduced into gardens at least 50 years ago—but I think it's better to simply define heirlooms as older garden varieties and, in particular, as those that are becoming hard to find and are in danger of being lost forever.

Even if history bores you to tears and you'd never hang an antique quilt in your 21st-century home, there's a good chance you'll find bulbs from the past that you will love. Here are my top eight reasons why.

Heirlooms are tough and easy. It's not surprising that heirloom bulbs are still with us decades or even centuries after many of their peers have vanished. They're usually tough, vigorous, disease-resistant, and adaptable to a wide variety of garden conditions. Think about it—if the jaunty 'Campernelle' narcissus, for example, has endured in gardens for more 400 years, isn't there a good chance it will last a good while in your garden too?

Heirlooms are unusual and distinct. If you like gardening with plants that are different, look to the past. Many heirloom bulbs offer unique features that newer varieties have not been able to match. There are crown imperials with gold-edged leaves, gloriously fragrant tulips (best of all, 'Prince of Austria'), perfect trumpet daffodils a few inches tall, and hyacinths that are virtually black. Heirloom bulbs can help transform your garden from humdrum to unique.

Bred for gardens rather than pot culture, antique hyacinths are richly fragrant. 'Marie' is dark indigo-purple; 'General Kohler' has double bells of blue-purple.

Heirlooms are often rich in fragrance. Fragrance is hard to breed for and not a top priority for most hybridizers, so it often disappears in newer introductions. Heirloom bulbs, however, are often powerfully fragrant. Hyacinths, lilies, daffodils (*Narcissus*), and the old white *Freesia alba* head the list, but there are others to be discovered by gardeners with an adventurous nose.

Heirlooms are a lot like wildflowers. Many of them have an informal grace and natural charm—and with good reason. The oldest heirloom bulbs are simply wildflowers—though no longer wild-collected, of course—and the earliest selections and crosses that ancient gardeners made from those natural gems.

Heirlooms are often regionally adapted. The vast majority of mainstream bulbs sold in North America today are raised in the cool temperate climate of the Netherlands. Many of these will fail in more challenging niches, especially in the South, but with a little effort you can find heirloom bulbs that will thrive for you, no matter where you garden. In fact, many are thriving in old gardens all around you, though they may be all but impossible to find at modern, mass-market sources.

Heirlooms are genetically diverse and unique. Genetic diversity is our best hope for breeding plants that will meet future needs, be they in food crops or ornamental plants. In order to develop tough, unusual bulbs for the widest diversity of challenges—and individual tastes—we can't afford to squander the rich genetic inheritance of heirlooms.

20 Great Heirloom Bulbs

CROCUSES

'Cloth of Gold' (*C. angustifolius*)—1587, the old "Turkey crocus"; bees flock to it.

'Negro Boy'—circa 1910, the name is an unfortunate relic, but the cultivar is the darkest crocus ever, midnight-purple.

C. tommasinianus—1847, lavender wildling, rated "most rodent-resistant."

DAFFODILS

'Butter and Eggs'—1777, yellow and gold double, a folk favorite.

'Campernelle'—1601, thrives in Southern gardens that have been abandoned for centuries.

'Conspicuus'—1869, Victorian landmark, graceful as a butterfly.

'Early Louisiana' jonquil—1612, its sweet fragrance is the essence of spring.

'Irene Copeland'—1915, primrose-and-ivory, perfect for an Easter bonnet.

'Mrs. R.O. Backhouse'—1921, the first "pink" daffodil, luscious apricot trumpet.

'Seagull'—1893, snow-white wings, lemon cup kissed with orange.

'W.P. Milner'—1869, elfin miniature, silvery yellow nodding trumpets.

HYACINTHS

'General Kohler'—1878, luxuriant double bells of blue-purple.

'Marie'—1860, deep, dark indigo-purple and richly fragrant.

'Prinses Maria Christina'—1948, soft peach with gold highlights.

'Butter and Eggs', a long-loved double daffodil, has been in cultivation since 1777.

TULIPS

'Clara Butt'—1889, undisputed queen for decades, now all but lost.

Lady tulip (*T. clusiana*)—1607, tough but dainty white-and-rose wildflower.

'Philippe de Comines'—1891, as dark and rich as polished mahogany.

'Prince of Austria'—1860, powerfully fragrant and enduring.

'Willem van Oranje'—1933, peach and copper double, as if painted by Renoir.

'Zomerschoon'—1620, exquisite relic of Tulipomania, pricey but priceless.

It's easy to help save endangered garden plants: Just grow them. Heirloom varieties that fall out of favor risk being lost forever. Above are two heirloom tulips: *Tulipa clusiana* at left, and 'Willem van Oranje' at right.

Heirlooms are endangered and in need of your help! Rainforest rarities are not the only unique, irreplaceable plants that are being lost forever. Every year an incredible array of endangered garden plants is slipping through our fingers. One sobering example: In the 1800s, when dahlias ranked right up there with roses in popularity, some 10,000 named, distinct cultivars were introduced. Today only three of these survive. Though we may not be able to save the giant panda in our own backyard, we can all help with endangered garden plants. Just grow them. It's the only way to save them.

Best of all, heirlooms root us. In the same way that old photos hanging on the wall can make us feel more deeply the bonds we share with friends and family, heirloom bulbs in the garden can help root us in a timeless community of gardeners. Your dahlia-loving grandfather, the young woman who planted daffodils at your house ages ago, and even Thomas Jefferson or Empress Josephine—you can bring them all into your garden by growing heirloom bulbs. I don't know anything else that can add to your garden more pleasure or emotional power.

Enrich your garden, touch the past, and help save an irreplaceable inheritance.

CHEAPER BY THE DOZEN:
Bulb Propagation Made Simple

ALESSANDRO CHIARI

I t's easy to increase your supply of true bulbs, corms, and rhizomes by using a slightly different propagation method for each. The most common way to increase bulbous plants is by vegetative, or asexual, propagation, which means propagation from a part of the plant other than its seeds. Vegetative propagation, unlike propagation from seed, also ensures that the resulting plants will be identical to the mother plant.

Propagating True Bulbs

During its life cycle a true bulb produces daughter bulbs called bulblets, or off-sets, which replace the mother bulb when it dies. In many bulbous plants this happens once the mother bulb has produced a flowering stem. If you pull up a tulip after flowering, you will see that the bulb that gave rise to the flower stem is completely spent and that a few small bulbs—the bulblets—are attached at the base

of the stem. Taking advantage of their fascinating underground life, it's easy to propagate true bulbs: When the foliage has died down, gently lift the bulbs and separate the bulblets. Replant them immediately in a nursery area or where you want new plants to grow.

Propagating true bulbs is easy: Separate the bulblets from the mother bulb and plant them where you'd like new plants to grow. Shown here is a bulb of grape hyacinth, *Muscari armeniacum*, with bulblets.

Top and bottom: Making more hyacinths by scooping: Remove the basal plate from a dormant bulb, and in two to three months bulblets will form.

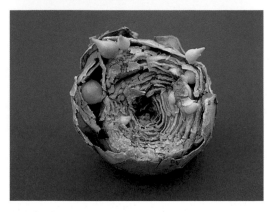

The bulblets will sprout the following growing season and will use the energy captured by their leaves to reach flowering size, a process that may take from one to three years.

Some bulb species such as hyacinths don't produce many off-sets on their own and require scoring or scooping, two fancier propagation techniques that should also be done in summer, when the bulbs are dormant.

To *score* a bulb, take a sharp knife and make three straight cuts across the base of the bulb and about halfway up (to bulb "hip" level). The bulb should hold together, but its base should be divided into six equal sections, resembling pie slices. Store the bulb upside down in a warm place in the dark or in diffused light. For example, place the scored bulb upside down in a cup or small container and keep it on a shelf or inside a cabinet. In about two to three months small bulblets will develop near the wounds.

To *scoop* a bulb, you need to remove its basal plate, at the wider end, fully exposing the bases of the scale leaves, the small fleshy leaves compressed inside where food is stored. A sharp knife will work fine, but you can make the perfect bulb-scooping tool by filing the edge of a teaspoon until it's sharp. Once you've removed the base, store the bulb upside down in a warm place, as discussed above for scoring. Small bulblets will appear on the wounded bulb scales in about two to three months.

Separate the bulblets you've obtained through scoring or scooping from the mother bulb and plant them out in a nursery area in the fall. As these bulblets are rather small and fragile, most gardeners simply plant the mother bulb upside down with the bulblets still attached. Don't expect the bulblets to produce flowers in the next growing season though, it takes several years before they reach flowering size.

Propagating Corms

The corms of spring-flowering bulbous plants are usually very small and have the tendency to be buried deep in the soil. As it's difficult to unearth them unharmed, propagating spring-flowering corms is a challenge. The life cycle of a corm is not very different from that of a true bulb. Corms produce daughter corms called cormels, which you can separate from the main corm once it goes dormant. Lift out corms such as crocuses when the foliage has turned yellow, separate the cormels and replant them right away, either in their final location or in a nursery area. If replanting immediately is impractical, you can store the cormels in saw-dust until fall.

Propagating Rhizomes

Rhizomes are underground stems that grow horizontally. Gardeners usually propagate rhizomes through division. To do this, cut the rhizome into sections,

To propagate iris rhizomes, cut off sections that have at least one bud and plant them.

making sure that each piece has at least one of the easily located buds, or growing points. Irises, one of the most common rhizomes in the garden, are propagated in summer, at the end of their flowering period. Dig out the rhizomes and discard the old growth, which does not bear any leaves. Keep the rhizome sections that bear leaves (usually called "fan leaves" because of the way they fan out). The sections should be about 3 to 4 inches long. Replant them at the same depth they were planted before and cut the fan leaves back to about 6 inches above the ground.

KEEPING YOUR SPRING BULBS HEALTHY:

A Diagnostic Guide to Pests and Diseases

BETH HANSON

Spring bulbs emerge, bloom, and go dormant before it's warm enough for many pests and diseases to kick into action. They are susceptible to some insect and disease problems, though, and the best way to keep these at bay is to exercise care when choosing, siting, and planting bulbs. See "An Ounce of Prevention," page 49.

The following guide will help you determine what is ailing your bulbs and decide on a course of action. Organized by plant symptoms, it provides an overview of the possible culprits of bulb decline and briefly explains the least toxic control options available for each.

Examine your plants closely, and once you've diagnosed a problem that needs treatment, choose one of the least toxic control options, since these are the least harmful to your garden and all its inhabitants. To help diagnose bulb problems, also refer to local resources, including your county extension service or a nearby botanical garden, which may provide a plant diagnostic service. For more advice on plant problems and the least toxic treatment options, see Brooklyn Botanic Garden handbooks *Natural Insect Control* and *Natural Disease Control*.

Symptom: Yellowing Leaves

POSSIBLE CAUSE: APHIDS

Tiny pear-shaped insects, aphids congregate on the stems, leaves, or roots of plants, where they suck sap. They attack most types of bulbs but have a slight preference for lilies and begonias.
Symptoms of infestation also include stunted and deformed leaves and stems, and

By selecting, siting, and planting bulbs carefully, you will be able to avoid most pest and disease problems.

plant parts covered with honeydew, a sticky, sugary substance. As they feed, aphids spread diseases from plant to plant, including viruses such as the "breaking," or mosaic virus that attacks tulips and lilies, giving rise to the bizarre petals of broken tulips.

To control: Spray plants with jets of water, or wipe with a cotton swab dipped in rubbing alcohol or a mild solution of dishwashing detergent and water.

POSSIBLE CAUSE: MEALYBUGS

These small, white, wingless insects are sapsuckers, and like aphids feed on the leaves, stems, roots, and flowers of a range of plants. They appear most often in warm, humid weather. If the infestation is heavy, leaves will yellow, plants will be stunted, and flower and fruit size will be diminished.

To control: Remove and kill mealybugs and waxy egg sacs with a solution of 70 percent rubbing alcohol. Lady beetles, particularly the larvae of *Cryptolaemus montrouzieri,* are very effective predators.

POSSIBLE CAUSE: BASAL ROT

Basal rot attacks narcissus and members of the genus *Allium* (onions), causing bulbs to soften and rot: Mold may cover the base; leaves will yellow, then brown, and eventually drop; stems can droop and may have brown streaking on the inside. Plants often die. The *Fusarium* fungus that causes the disease can persist in the soil for many years.

To control: Remove and destroy infected plant parts. Choose resistant varieties, and don't plant bulbs in an area you believe may be affected.

Symptom: Notches or Holes in Leaves

POSSIBLE CAUSE: SNAILS AND SLUGS

Both snails and slugs consume seedlings and soft-tissued plant parts. Both feed at night and on cloudy, damp days and leave shiny slime trails. Slugs eat large holes in leaves, sometimes defoliating entire plants. Snails create irregular holes in the middle or at the edges of leaves. Both like many types of bulbs but often prefer gladioli and lilies.

To control: Locate and eliminate dark, damp spots where slugs and snails hide. Handpick daily, then weekly when numbers drop. Homemade traps, such as boards raised just above soil level are effective lures; snails and sometimes slugs gather underneath. Saucers filled with beer may also attract slugs; empty them daily. Set copper strips around tree trunks or raised beds. Diatomaceous earth is also effective against slugs and snails.

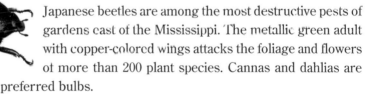

POSSIBLE CAUSE: JAPANESE BEETLES

Japanese beetles are among the most destructive pests of gardens east of the Mississippi. The metallic green adult with copper-colored wings attacks the foliage and flowers of more than 200 plant species. Cannas and dahlias are preferred bulbs.

To control: Handpick adults and control larvae with beneficial nematodes or the bacteria milky spore.

Symptom: Mottled or Streaked Leaves

POSSIBLE CAUSE: BULB MITES

These tiny pests puncture the foliage of a variety of bulbous plants and feed on sap. They are so tiny that they may not be detectable without a hand lens. Infestation can cause yellowish or silvery leaves; severe yellowing and rusty spots may follow. Fine silk webbing may also cover leaves and stems. Mites can spread bacteria and fungi from plant to plant.

To control: Wash plants with a mild detergent and rinse with water. Remove and destroy heavily infested parts. Insecticidal soaps provide some control.

POSSIBLE CAUSE: NEMATODES

These microscopic wormlike creatures feed on the roots, leaves, and stems of many plants. Symptoms of nematode infestation include mottling, streaking, or stunted, yellow leaves and wilting plants during hot periods. Nematodes spread readily in water and on garden tools.

To control: Pull up infested plants and destroy them. Send a soil sample to your local extension office for nematode identification. Treat the soil with organic fertilizers and amendments containing seaweed and humic acids. Grow resistant bulb varieties.

POSSIBLE CAUSE: THRIPS

Thrips are tiny insects that feed on the foliage of gladioli and onions (*Allium*), making long, thin cuts in the process. The plant takes on a streaked, dull, grayish cast called "silvering." Onion thrips are pale yellow tinged with black; gladiolus thrips are brownish black.

To control: Use sticky yellow traps. Spray plants often with water, or in severe cases, with insecticidal soap. Clean up host plants after the first frost.

Symptom: Plants Fail to Emerge or Are Stunted and Grow Slowly

POSSIBLE CAUSE: WIREWORMS

Wireworms are most common in the West but can be found throughout North America. The white or yellow worms are the larval stage of brown to black beetles. Wireworms are most active in warm, moist soil, and consume onions, gladioli, dahlias, and other plants, chewing narrow tunnels into roots and tubers and creating a point of entry for decay.

To control: Avoid planting where turf has grown in the past year. Handpick all stages. Bury roots or tubers of a susceptible crop such as carrots or potatoes as lures, then dig them and discard them with the worms. Apply commercially available beneficial nematodes to the soil.

POSSIBLE CAUSE: NARCISSUS FLIES

Narcissus flies attack amaryllis, snowdrops (*Galanthus*), snowflakes (*Leucojum*), hyacinths, and narcissus by laying eggs in plants' necks. Foliage soon withers. Larvae eat the center of the bulb, and plants fail to emerge the following season. Adults resemble bumblebees.

To control: Remove and destroy affected plants.

Symptom: Gray Mold on Foliage

POSSIBLE CAUSE: DOWNY MILDEW

Downy mildew is a fungal disease that causes white to purple downy growths along stems and on the undersides of leaves, with corresponding yellow spots above. Plants may succumb rapidly to the disease.

To control: Promote air circulation by spacing plants adequately. Destroy infected plant parts. Grow resistant varieties.

POSSIBLE CAUSE: BOTRYTIS BLIGHT

A fungal disease that attacks a number of bulbs such as lilies, snowdrops, anemones, and tulips, *Botrytis* blight appears as a white or gray fluffy growth, then causes stems to weaken. It can also cause yellow or brown spots on leaves. *Botrytis* spreads via splashing water and wind.

To control: Pick off and destroy infected leaves or remove and destroy infected plants. Promote air circulation around plants and water early in the day so plants can dry off.

Encyclopedia of
Spring-Blooming Bulbs

C. COLSTON BURRELL AND LUCY HARDIMAN

On the following pages you will find portraits of more than 50 popular and unusual spring-blooming bulbs for your garden. Browse through this section to discover what these plants look like, what they need to thrive, and how to best integrate them into a spring garden. Please refer to "A Step-by-Step Guide: Growing Bulbs Successfully," starting on page 16, for a closer look at year-round bulb care. A map of the USDA hardiness zones appears on page 101.

Opposite: Reticulated iris, *Iris reticulata*.

~~um~~ unifolium
~~RNAMENTAL ONION~~

Close to 700 species populate this genus most often identified with garlic, onions, chives, shallots, and leeks, key ingredients in kitchens the world over. Like their flavor-enhancing brethren, ornamental onions display a number of star- or bell-shaped flowers assembled in umbels. The grasslike, strappy foliage releases a distinctive onion scent when crushed. Spring-blooming *Allium* species are generally shorter in stature and have less dramatic flowers than later-blooming species, but they are alluring and subtle additions to the spring garden. *A. unifolium* is happiest in moist soils. The grassy foliage withers as the purple-pink flowers appear in late spring on 12- to 18-inch stalks.

NATIVE HABITAT Pacific Northwest

HARDINESS ZONES 5 to 10

HOW TO GROW Alliums tolerate soil conditions ranging from poor and sandy to more fertile and clayey, but they appreciate a site in full sun with good drainage and can tolerate dry soil. The smaller species look best when planted in clumps, with bulbs spaced 3 to 6 inches apart.

CULTIVARS AND RELATED SPECIES *Allium neopolitanum,* Naples, or daffodil, garlic stands 6 to 12 inches tall and bears loose umbels of fragrant white flowers. *A. roseum* features rose-pink clusters of star-shaped flowers on 12- to 16-inch stems. They are good cut flowers. *A. triquetrum,* the three-cornered leek, thrives in partial shade and moist soil, where it will naturalize. Flowers are white and bell-shaped with green stripes, borne in nodding clusters on 9- to 15-inch stems. Known as wood garlic, *A. ursinum* prefers partial shade and damp soil. Pristine white starlike flowers in flat umbels exude a strong garlic fragrance. All are hardy in Zones 3 to 9.

COMPANION PLANTS Clusters of *A. unifolium* are charming interplanted with lady's mantle (*Alchemilla*), and wallflowers (*Erysimum*) for a cottage-garden flavor. The unique coloration of *A. triquetrum* brightens the shady border when combined with white-variegated hostas, white primroses (*Primula*), ferns, and white hellebores.   *—LH*

Anemone blanda
GRECIAN WINDFLOWER

These white "daisies" of early spring are beloved by gardeners for their pristine elegance. Flowers with single rings of up to a dozen petals open one to a stem above a triad of ferny, lobed

Spring-flowering ornamental onions are more delicate than many later-blooming varieties. At left is *Allium unifolium.*

leaves. Plants bloom as they emerge from the warming soil and reach 3 to 4 inches when mature.

NATIVE HABITAT Open woods and rocky slopes of the eastern Mediterranean

HARDINESS ZONES 4 (with protection) to 8

HOW TO GROW The tubers of windflower arrive looking like shriveled muscat raisins, seemingly without hope of survival. Before planting, soak them overnight in warm water to rehydrate. It is almost impossible to tell which end is up, so don't even try. Set tubers 1 to 2 inches below the surface of humus-rich, evenly moist soil in full sun or light shade. Deep planting, 3 to 4 inches, is recommended in northern zones. After flowering, plants go dormant and are tolerant of dry conditions. Heavy wet soil in summer may rot the tubers. Where plants are happy, they will spread to form dense, floriferous clumps that seldom need division.

Soak the shriveled-looking tubers of Grecian windflower before planting.

CULTIVARS AND RELATED SPECIES
Anemone blanda 'Blue Shades' varies in color from medium to deep purple-blue; 'Charmer' is deep rosy pink; 'Pink Star' has large, medium pink flowers; 'Radar' is vibrant fuchsia with a white eye; 'Violet Star' is medium rosy violet; 'White Splendor' has daisy-like, snow-white flowers. Zones 4 to 8. *A. coronaria,* poppy anemone, has gorgeous blood-red, black-centered flowers above leaves that resemble curly parsley. The species is seldom available commercially, but a number of outstanding selections in single or mixed colors, such as the pure white 'The Bride', scarlet 'The Governor', and violet 'Mister Fokker' are readily available for spring or fall planting. Zones 7 to 9. *A. pavonina* and its hybrid *A.* × *fulgens* have flaming

scarlet flowers on 1-foot stems in late spring. Though scarce in cultivation, they are worth seeking out for a summer dry spot in full sun or light shade. Zones 6 to 9. Some *Anemone* species are collected from the wild. For more information on the problems of wild collection and what to look for when purchasing bulbs, see "Buyer Beware," on page 14.

COMPANION PLANTS Windflowers consort happily with most plants in woodlands, borders, and rock gardens. Combine white-flowered selections with blue lungwort (*Pulmonaria*), Jacob's ladder *(Polemonium reptans),* and bold-leafed bishop's hat *Epimedium sagittatum.* Blue-flowered selections contrast beautifully with white daffodils, 'Maroon Velvet' primroses (*Primula*), and milk-chocolate gaudy jack (*Arisaema sikokianum*), In a rockery, choose species tulips such as scarlet *T. sprengeri,* cranesbills (*Geranium*), rhododendrons, and dwarf conifers. —*CB*

...emone nemorosa

...OOD ANEMONE, WINDFLOWER

Wood anemone is a lovely and easily grown species that forms tight carpets of ferny foliage studded with ½- to 1-inch starry white flowers like a galaxy that fell to earth. Emerging plants resemble tiny spidery aliens with oversize heads. The globular buds open to reveal five to eight white petallike sepals, often blushed pink on the reverse. A triad of deeply lobed leaves rings the 4- to 8-inch stems just below the flowers, which last for a week or so in early spring.

NATIVE HABITAT Open woodlands and shaded roadsides from Britain and northern Europe to Turkey

HARDINESS ZONES 4 to 8

HOW TO GROW Plant the thin, sticklike rhizomes 1 inch below the surface in humus-rich, evenly moist soil in a sunny to partially shaded spot. Plants go dormant soon after flowering. In just a few years the rhizomes form tightly congested, interwoven clumps that should be divided to keep plants

vigorous and free-flowering. Lift them as the foliage is yellowing, pull the brittle rhizomes apart, and replant.

CULTIVARS AND RELATED SPECIES
Anemone nemorosa 'Allenii' has large lavender flowers; 'Bowles' Purple' has crisp-looking blue-purple flowers; 'Bracteata Pleniflora' has flattened, fully double white and green flowers with narrow petals; 'Lychette' has huge white flowers that fade to pink; 'Vestal' is pure white with a pompon center; 'Virescens' has a mop of spidery green bracts replacing the petals. All are hardy in Zones 4 to 8. *A. apennina,* Apennine windflower, is a lovely, slow-creeping species with daisylike 1½-inch flowers with a double ring of 10 to 18 petals. Plants grow 6 to 8 inches tall with a triad of fuzzy, divided leaves. Zones 4 to 7. *A. ranunculoides,* buttercup anemone, has a growth pattern similar to that of wood anemone. Bright buttercup-yellow half-inch flowers cover the fresh green clumps. 'Pleniflora' has semi- to fully double flowers. Zones 4 to 8. *A.* × *lipsiensis* is a charming hybrid between the buttercup and wood anemones with flowers intermediate in color. Overall a more delicate plant, its 1-inch creamy-buttermilk-yellow flowers open on stems to 4 inches tall. Zones 4 to 8.

COMPANION PLANTS Wood anemones spread to form a tight groundcover and look best in the company of tall plants. Contrast the white flowers with deep purple or maroon hellebores, purple toad trillium (*Trillium cuneatum*), and Virginia bluebell (*Mertensia virginica*). Let them trail among the open stems of shrubs such as winter hazel

Within a few years wood anemones spread to form a tight groundcover.

Growing from clustered tuberous roots, North American native rue anemones can be divided after flowering every few years.

(*Corylopsis*), daphne (*Daphne odora* 'Variegata'), and witch alder (*Fothergilla gardenii*). Anemones go dormant after flowering, so mix them with ferns, Solomon's seal (*Polygonatum*), and other plants that emerge after the bulbs have flowered.   —*CB*

Anemonella (Thalictrum) thalictroides
RUE ANEMONE

The wiry stems of rue anemone tremble in the slightest breeze, giving rise to the romantic name windflower. Plants produce multiple stems crowned with open clusters of white to pale pink flowers above a triad of three-lobed leaves resembling the medicinal herb rue (*Ruta graveolens*) and meadow rue (*Thalictrum*), from which it gets its specific name *thalictroides*.

NATIVE HABITAT Open, rocky woods and roadsides from New Hampshire and Minnesota south to Florida and Kansas

HARDINESS ZONES 3 to 8

HOW TO GROW Plant rue anemone in humus-rich, well-drained soil in light to partial shade. Plants grow from clustered tuberous roots that can be divided after flowering, keeping a bud to each division. Reset the tubers no more than an inch below the soil surface. Double-flowered selections tend to increase quickly, and the crowded tubers will rot if not divided every two to three years. Plants flower for a month or so in spring, then slip quietly into dormancy in summer.

CULTIVARS AND RELATED SPECIES *Anemonella thalictroides* 'Betty Blake', also sold as 'Green Dragon', has starry double apple-green flowers. 'Cameo' is a soft shell-pink double that fades to near white. 'Schoaf's Double Pink' is a lovely deep rose pompon.

COMPANION PLANTS Rue anemones are delicate, so don't overpower them with thuggish or garish companions. Place them close to the path, on a slope, or in a raised rockery where they are easily appreciated. Use them s for maximum impact, along shooting star (*Dodecatheon ...dia*), smaller epimediums such E. × *youngianum*, and fragile fern *Cystopteris protrusa*).   —CB

Arisaema candidissimum
WHITE JACK

The flowers of most jack-in-the-pulpits are more curious than beautiful, but the white-and-pink-striped spathe of white jack is truly stunning. The unique flower construction features a tubular, flared spathe with a flipped-up tip like a 1950s pompadour haircut and a clublike spadix rising from the center. Plants bloom in late spring or

Later in the season, white jack will produce decorative red berries and self-seed.

summer, long after most jacks have faded. The single, three-lobed leaf emerges with or after the flowers.

NATIVE HABITAT Wooded slopes and moist forests of western China

HARDINESS ZONES 5 to 9

HOW TO GROW Give jacks rich, evenly moist but well-drained soil in partial to full shade. Plant the dormant tubers in

spring or late autumn, or set out containerized plants when available. Plants will self-sow from decorative orange or red berries.

CULTIVARS AND RELATED SPECIES
Arisaema ringens, cobra jack, sports an oversize flared, pinstriped hood that hides the spadix. A pair of huge, three-lobed glossy leaves towers above the flowers. Zones 6 to 9. *A. sikokianum,* gaudy jack, has luscious dark-chocolate flowers with a knobby snow-white spathe. The five- to seven-part leaves are often mottled with silver and sit below the flower. Zones 4 (with protection) to 9. *A. triphyllum* is the native American jack with a smartly hooded, open spathe striped with green or deep purple. Paired, three-lobed leaves are held above the flower. Zones 3 to 9.

COMPANION PLANTS Jacks lend an exotic flair to shaded gardens when jutting decoratively through a groundcover of barrenwort (*Epimedium*), ferns, and sedges. Plant them in clusters of three or more for maximum impact.   —CB

Arisarum proboscideum
MOUSE PLANT

Mouse plant is a curious little plant that looks like a huddle of mice feeding on a choice bit of cheese. The mouse in the common name arose from the slender, taillike tip to the tiny curved spathe, which may be 7 inches long. Plants produce rounded to arrow-shaped bright green leaves from fleshy, creeping rhizomes.

NATIVE HABITAT Open woodlands and scrub from Spain to Italy

HARDINESS ZONES 7 to 9

HOW TO GROW Plant in evenly moist, well-drained rich soil in partial to full shade. Plants go dormant in summer and are drought- and heat-tolerant.

CULTIVARS AND RELATED SPECIES
Pinellia cordata, miniature green dragon, is another small aroid related to mouse plant with tiny arrowhead-shaped deep green leaves decoratively mottled with creamy white. The undersides of the leaves are stained greenish purple. Zones 5 to 7. *P. tripartita* resembles a jack-in-the-pulpit in foliage but has small green flowers with long protruding upright tongues. This plant may be invasive in some areas. Zones 6 to 9.

COMPANION PLANTS Because it is so diminutive and so ephemeral, mouse plant looks best when grown as a specimen or groundcover, overplanted with a delicate groundcover such as sweet woodruff (*Galium odoratum*) or planted en masse around late-emerging ferns or hostas that will hide the blank spot left when plants go dormant in summer.   —*CB*

Arum italicum
ITALIAN ARUM
The mottled arrowhead leaves of Italian arum add life to the dull winter garden. Though there are four sub-species in the wild, the mottled forms of *A. italicum* subsp. *italicum* are most commonly grown. The leaves are produced in the fall, persist through the winter, and disappear after flowering the next summer. Showy orange-red berries are borne in dense clusters in late summer before the new leaves emerge. Plants grow from buttonlike tubers and spread slowly by short offsets to form dense clumps. Be aware that the species is beginning to show up on invasive-species watch lists in Oregon and may be invasive in other areas.

Italian arum is grown primarily for its foliage but bears dense clusters of orange-red berries in late summer.

NATIVE HABITAT Scrub and rocky woods around the Mediterranean to North Africa

HARDINESS ZONES 5 to 10

HOW TO GROW Plant in rich, evenly moist well-drained soil in light to partial shade. Will tolerate dense summer shade if there is winter sun while plants are actively growing. You can allow the soil to become dry without ill effect in summer when plants are leafless.

CULTIVARS AND RELATED SPECIES
Arum italicum 'Pictum' is a name applied to a number of heavily mottled individuals, most of which are seedlings of 'Marmoratum', which is a robust, heavily mottled selection of *A. italicum* subsp. *italicum*. *A. creticum* has beautiful fragrant yellow spathes that resemble a slender calla lily and unmarked arrowhead leaves. Zones 6 to 9. *Arum dioscoridis* has a large ill-scented purple-mottled spathe with an erect, deep purple spadix borne

among handsome large leaves. Zones 8 to 10.

COMPANION PLANTS Combinations should accentuate the superb foliage and fruit. Use the handsome mottled foliage to echo yellow colors of the winter garden such as yellow-twig dogwood (*Cornus stolonifera* 'Flaviramea') and green-flowered hellebores (*Helleborus odorus*). For contrast, try purple-leafed coral bells (*Heuchera* 'Plum Pudding'). Set the berries against a background of lush ferns. —*CB*

Bellevalia paradoxa

Colorful drifts of *Bellevalia* flowing under deciduous shrubs and between perennials add touches of color to the ground in early spring. Strap-shaped basal foliage is greenish gray and topped by 12-inch flower stalks. The bell-shaped, six-lobed flowers of *Bellevalia paradoxa* are arrayed in tight conical clusters of deep blue rimmed in yellow. Closely related to both grape hyacinths (*Muscari*), with which they are often confused, and

hyacinths (*Hyacinthus*), *Bellevalia* is relatively unknown to American gardeners, and the bulbs may be difficult to locate.

NATIVE HABITAT Mediterranean to western Asia

HARDINESS ZONES 7 to 9

HOW TO GROW Plant bulbs in autumn 2 inches below the surface in well-drained, amended soil in light shade or full sun. They are happy planted under deciduous trees where they receive full sun in the spring and little or no water after they go dormant in early summer. Divide clumps in early summer as the leaves begin to wither and die. Propagate plants by seed, division, or by separating offsets.

CULTIVARS AND RELATED SPECIES Formerly known as *Hyacinthus romanus*, *Bellevalia romana* bears small, milky-white bells tinged with green, which emit a light fragrance. *B. hyacinthoides* (originally named *Strangweja spicata*) develops strappy green foliage in fall and winter followed in spring by bloom stalks holding light blue loose racemes of bell-shaped flowers on 6-inch stems.

COMPANION PLANTS Mass groups of blue-flowering *Bellevalia* with the emerging chartreuse-hued foliage of Japanese forest grass (*Hakonechloa macra* 'Aureola') or Bowles golden grass (*Carex elata* 'Aurea') for high contrast. White-blooming species show up best in light shade with hostas, ferns, lungwort (*Pulmonaria*), and hellebores. Use them in combination with species tulips in containers, at the edge of a border, or in the rock garden. —*LH*

Bellevalia paradoxa is rarely cultivated in North American gardens, and the bulbs can be hard to find.

Ranging in color from pale to deep blue, the funnel-shaped flowers of *Brimeura amethystina* are a lure for butterflies.

Brimeura amethystina

The funnel-shaped, six-lobed flowers of *Brimeura amethystina* range in color from pale to deep blue and are a lure for butterflies. The blooms of this petite and delicate bluebell look-alike appear in May on leafless stalks rising 6 inches above grassy foliage. *Brimeura* is a genus of two species in the lily family that has been separated from its close relative *Hyacinthus*.

NATIVE HABITAT Meadows of southeastern Europe

HARDINESS ZONES 5 to 9

HOW TO GROW *Brimeura* grows best in well-drained, rich soil in part shade or full sun provided the bulbs are sheltered from high summer's afternoon sun; it is a good choice for planting beneath deciduous trees. Plant in clusters, spacing bulbs 6 to 8 inches apart; the top of the bulb should be 2 inches below the soil surface. Divide in summer after the leaves begin to die back, or propagate from seed.

CULTIVARS AND RELATED SPECIES *Brimeura amethystina* var. *alba* is white-flowered. Zones 5 to 9.

COMPANION PLANTS Although small in stature, *Brimeura* is dramatic in bloom when massed as a carpet underneath deciduous shrubs and trees. Use it to extend the bloom season by mingling it with earlier-blooming snowdrops in combination with hellebores, lungwort (*Pulmonaria*), and primroses (*Primula*).　　—LH

Bulbocodium vernum
SPRING MEADOW SAFFRON

Though not as showy as a hybrid crocus, this plant is quietly endearing. Elongated corms give rise to rich rosy-purple flowers that seem to be resting on the ground. The flowers have multiple ragged petals like a semidouble

61

When the flowers of spring meadow saffron fade, its strap-shaped leaves emerge and persist until early summer.

Colchicum, to which the plant is related. As the flowers fade, strappy leaves to 6 inches long emerge and persist until early summer.

NATIVE HABITAT Sunny alpine meadows and rocky slopes of south-central Europe

HARDINESS ZONES 3 to 8

HOW TO GROW This hardy plant thrives in rich, well-drained soil in full sun to partial shade. Plants need ample spring moisture but tolerate summer drought while dormant. Plant bulbs in drifts of a dozen to give the flowers more visual impact.

CULTIVARS AND RELATED SPECIES The second species of the genus, *Bulbodicum versicolor,* is only rarely grown.

COMPANION PLANTS Spring meadow saffron needs a spot where it can show off its subtle charms. I planted a group atop a rock outcropping where the flowers look great contrasted with the gray granite surface. Place them close to a path or atop a raised wall and group the bulbs closely together for maximum impact.   *—CB*

Calochortus venustus
WHITE MARIPOSA LILY

Few bulbs are as beautiful in bloom or as challenging to grow outside their native range as the wildflowers in the genus *Calochortus,* which can be found in arid areas of the western United States and Mexico. White mariposa lily, native along the Pacific coast and the Sierra Nevada Mountains, is one of the most variable of the bunch, displaying open-faced, cup-shaped flowers in late spring that range in color from white and yellow to pink and lilac. The bulbs were once a food source for Native Americans.

NATIVE HABITAT California, Utah, and Mexico

Calochortus venustus, a dryland plant that likes mild winters, is difficult to grow outside its native range.

HARDINESS ZONES 6 to 10

HOW TO GROW All *Calochortus* species are dryland plants native to areas that experience warm, dry summers and mild winters with low rainfall and little freezing and thawing. They prefer full sun and very well drained gritty soil rich in organic matter. Outside their native range, try them in rock gardens, in containers, in a bulb frame, or in an alpine house. In fall, set bulbs 4 to 6 inches deep. Propagate by sowing seed when ripe or by separating offsets.

CULTIVARS AND RELATED SPECIES The white bells of *Calochortus albus,* fairy lanterns, have inward-facing petals and a pendant habit. The sunny yellow blooms of *C. amabilis,* the golden globe tulip, are displayed in nodding clusters. *C. luteus* has slender stems and bright yellow flowers and sports an orange nectary at the base of the

The bulbs of North American native *Camassia leichtlinii* were once a food source. At right is 'Blue Danube'.

flower. *C. tolmiei*, cat's ears or pussy ears, have long hairs on the inner flower parts.

COMPANION PLANTS Partner *Calochortus* species with other native bulbs, bunch grasses, species forms of beard-tongues (*Penstemon*), wild buckwheats (*Eriogonum*), and sedums. —*LH*

Camassia leichtlinii
CAMASS

I would not want to be without this most stately species in a genus of gorgeous late-spring- to early-summer-flowering true bulbs. Racemes of starry pale to deep blue flowers rise to 3 feet tall above a whorl of glossy green leaves folded upward in the middle to form a V-shape. The fleshy bulbs were a food source for native people and early settlers.

NATIVE HABITAT Moist to wet meadows from Alberta and Utah west to British Columbia and California

HARDINESS ZONES 3 to 8

HOW TO GROW Plant in rich, evenly moist soil in full sun or light shade. If set in too much shade, plants will not rebloom. In the wild, the meadows where this plant grows are quite dry in summer, so moderate summer drought is not a problem, but bone-dry soil for extended periods will compromise the following year's flowers. Place the large bulbs 4 to 6 inches deep.

CULTIVARS AND RELATED SPECIES *Camassia leichtlinii* 'Alba' has creamy white flowers that glow when planted with blues. 'Blue Danube' is stunning, with deep indigo flowers on 3-foot stems. 'Semiplena' has double creamy-white flowers. *C. cusickii* has pale blue flowers on 2- to $2\frac{1}{2}$-foot stems. Zones 3 to 8. *C. quamash* is more delicate, with slender inflorescences to 2 feet tall and deep purple-blue flowers. 'Blue Melody' is coveted for its yellow-margined leaves contrasting with the richly colored flowers. Zones 3 to 8. *C. scilloides,* wild hyacinth, is the only eastern species, with icy to medium

blue flowers on 1- to 2-foot stems. Zones 4 to 8.

COMPANION PLANTS The tall spikes of camass are stunning in the spring garden protruding from a planting of cranesbills (*Geranium*), ferns, and the emerging leaves of meadow rue (*Thalictrum*). Group at least a dozen bulbs together, and plant several drifts for maximum impact. In more formal settings, combine them with masterwort (*Astrantia major*) and other moisture-loving perennials. Contrast the spiky inflorescences with the spherical heads of ornamental onions (*Allium*).   —CB

Cardamine (Dentaria) heptaphylla
TOOTHWORT
This and other European *Cardamine* species are far more eye-catching than their North American kin. Larger in all respects, the toothed, pinnately divided foliage and $^3/_4$-inch upward-facing white to pale pink flowers make a brief but glorious showing in spring.

NATIVE HABITAT Open woods and moist streamsides in southwestern Europe

HARDINESS ZONES 4 to 8

HOW TO GROW Toothworts are woodland denizens, so give them humus-rich, evenly moist soil in light to partial shade. After plants go dormant in late spring, they can tolerate shade and dry conditions. They are native to mountainous regions and are quite winter hardy. Plants spread by creeping, fleshy rhizomes to form broad clumps. Avoid planting them near dense groundcovers and aggressive spreaders that will crowd or smother these delicate beauties.

Woodland denizens, toothworts require humus-rich soil in light to partial shade.

Thriving under deciduous trees and shrubs in full sun in late winter and spring, glory-of-the-snow naturalizes easily and in time will form large clumps.

CULTIVARS AND RELATED SPECIES
Cardamine diphylla, crinkleroot, has bold foliage with broad oval leaflets and open clusters of nodding pale pink flowers. Zones 4 to 8. *C. laciniata,* cutleaf toothwort, is a favorite of wildflower enthusiasts. The foliage is cut into five to seven narrow, fingerlike divisions, and the white to pale pink flowers are ½ inch across. Zones 3 to 8. *C. pentaphylla,* showy toothwort, has large, deep pink buck-toothed flowers that dangle over three handsome toothed, handlike leaves. Zones 4 to 8.

COMPANION PLANTS Combine toothwort with early bulbs such as snowdrops (*Galanthus*), cyclamen, European wood anemone (*Anemone nemorosa*), and *Corydalis*. To fill the gaps in summer, choose persistent species such as Callaway wild ginger (*Asarum shuttleworthii* 'Callaway'), foamflower (*Tiarella*), hellebores, and clump-forming ferns.   —*CB*

Chionodoxa luciliae
GLORY-OF-THE-SNOW
In March and April, glory-of-the-snow puts forth small, star-shaped, upward-facing violet-blue flowers with white centers. Flowers are six-lobed and borne in racemes with six tepals each. Bulbs produce two to three narrow, straplike leaves. *Chionodoxa* is aptly named: "Chion" is Greek for snow, "doxa" means glory. In their native habitats these plants bloom in late winter and early spring as the snow is melting. *C. luciliae* (also known as. *C. gigantea)* is often confused with other species.

NATIVE HABITAT High alpine meadows in Turkey, Crete, and Cyprus

HARDINESS ZONES 3 to 9

HOW TO GROW Glory-of-the snow prefers well-drained soil in full sun or partial to full shade. The plants thrive under deciduous trees and shrubs that get full sun in late winter and spring when the bulbs are producing growth. Plant them in large groups of 25 to 50 in fall, 3 inches deep. They naturalize easily and in time will form their own large clumps. Dig and divide clumps as the foliage dies back in early summer.

CULTIVARS AND RELATED SPECIES *Chionodoxa luciliae* 'Alba' bears pure white flowers. *C. luciliae* 'Pink Giant' is soft pink with a white eye. Deep blue flowers on 8-inch stems are the hallmark of *C. forbesii*, a species that used to be commonly cultivated but is now rarely grown. All are hardy in Zones 3 to 9.

COMPANION PLANTS Although a fleeting presence, a carpet of glory-of-the-snow can be the subtle star of the spring garden. A soft tapestry of *C.* 'Pink Giant' enhances the deep, dusky shades of purple- and black-toned hellebores. Swathes of violet-blue glory-of-the snow contrast with the soft, buttery-yellow blooms of winter

hazel (*Corylopsis pauciflora*). Pools of glory-of-the snow among early species tulips or early-blooming *Narcissus* 'February Gold' add drama to the late-winter garden.   —*LH*

Claytonia virginica
SPRING-BEAUTY

The charming, delicate starry pink to white flowers of spring-beauty herald the arrival of spring in the deciduous forest. One of the first native wildflowers to bloom, it is also one of the last to fade, as it flowers nonstop for a month, then quietly slips into dormancy. The five-petaled flowers are often lined with deep pink, and the pollen is pink as well. Fleshy, narrow leaves are produced in abundance from a rounded tuberlike corm.

NATIVE HABITAT Open woods and floodplain forests throughout eastern and central North America

HARDINESS ZONES 3 to 8

HOW TO GROW Plant in moist, rich, loamy or humus-rich soil in light to full shade. Near-neutral to slightly acidic soil suits them best. The summer-dormant plants compete well with shallow tree roots, but they thrive best in deeper soils. When conditions are to their liking, plants self-sow freely to form extensive colonies.

CULTIVARS AND RELATED SPECIES *Claytonia caroliniana,* Carolina spring-beauty, is a more delicate plant with paired, elliptical leaves held below the open clusters of white to pink flowers. It thrives in humus-rich, acidic to near-neutral soil. Zones 4 to 8.

COMPANION PLANTS A delicate charmer, spring-beauty will weave artfully among taller plants such as

One of the first native wildflowers to bloom is spring-beauty.

daffodils (*Narcissus*), wake robins (*Trillium*), Virginia bluebells (*Mertensia virginica*), and ferns, filling all the gaps with its starry flowers. In the thin soil around shallow-rooted trees, combine it with cyclamens, scillas, and snowdrops (*Galanthus*). —*CB*

Convallaria majalis
LILY-OF-THE-VALLEY

Just a whiff of the sweet scent from the small, waxy, milky-white flowers of lily-of-the-valley conjures up memories of Grandma's garden. The dark green, ovate to rounded leaves emerge in early spring from fleshy rhizomes, which spread to form dense mats of perennial groundcover. The delicate, nodding, bell-shaped flowers are held in one-sided racemes on 9-inch stems.

NATIVE HABITAT Northern temperate zones in Europe, Asia, and North America

HARDINESS ZONES 2 to 8

HOW TO GROW Lilies-of-the-valley tolerate a variety of conditions ranging from deep shade to full sun. They prefer rich, evenly moist organic soil and some degree of protection from the strong rays of afternoon sun, but if watered well they can tolerate full sun. Older, established colonies are able to endure dry shade. In optimum conditions plants spread freely and can become quite aggressive. Frequent division helps slow them down and restrains their growth. Plant pips— bare root pieces of rhizome with a bud—in autumn, late winter, or spring 3 inches deep and at least 12 inches apart. In late summer cut tattered, weathered foliage to the ground. Divide colonies in early spring or fall and transplant as needed to control spread and to increase bloom.

The pink and variegated forms of lily-of-the-valley spread slowly, so put them in a spot where they are easy to see.

CULTIVARS AND RELATED SPECIES *Convallaria majalis* var. *rosea* displays pale mauve-pink flowers and 'Flore Pleno' has eye-catching, double white bells. Two striking variegated forms, 'Albostriata' with longitudinal white stripes and the yellow-striped 'Aureovariegata', are dramatic additions to the shade garden.

COMPANION PLANTS Lily-of-the-valley should be carefully sited well away from delicate spring ephemerals such as wake robins (*Trillium*) and dog-tooth violet (*Erythronium revolutum*), which could be easily overrun. Instead, plant them inside the drip line of deciduous and evergreen trees where they can ramble at will and become a solid mass of groundcover. The pink and variegated forms are slow to bulk up, so site them close to a walkway where you can appreciate their stunning beauty and luscious fragrance. —*LH*

Corydalis solida
FUME ROOT

If tales of the fussy blue fume root from China have made you timid about trying *Corydalis,* start with this easy, prolific species. Dense racemes of mauve flowers 3 to 4 inches tall are borne so profusely that the delicately dissected, blue-green leaves are barely visible. Plants self-sow freely and clumps increase rapidly, so a few bulbs soon turn into many. After flowering, the plant quickly fades away.

NATIVE HABITAT Woodlands from Scandinavia south to the Balkans

HARDINESS ZONES 4 to 8

Plant fume root around late-emerging perennials that will fill the gap when the spring bloomers go dormant.

HOW TO GROW It may be difficult to tell the top from the bottom of the yellow, rounded to somewhat hour-glass shaped tuberous roots. Look for the small circular scar on one of the long ends and set it downward 2 to 3 inches below the surface of rich, moist soil. In time, the tuberous roots, which are reformed each year on top of the old spent root from the previous year, work their way to the surface, so keep them covered with compost or periodically lift them and reset them 2 to 3 inches down.

CULTIVARS AND RELATED SPECIES *Corydalis solida* 'Beth Evans' has soft pink flowers of a clearer color than the wild form. 'George Baker' has gorgeous rose-red flowers that make more of an impact in the garden than the paler-colored species. *C. bulbosa* (*cava*) is a showy species with upright spikes of white flowers 4 to 5 inches tall. The dissected foliage is coarser than that of *C. solida*, and plants grow from persistent tubers. Zones 4 to 8.

COMPANION PLANTS Fume root works well planted around late-emerging perennials like hostas, peonies (*Paeonia*), and ferns that fill the gap left when the attractive spring bloomers go dormant. Plants will self-sow to fill gaps in a woodland or perennial border. Combine them with other early bulbs, wildflowers, and hellebores.   —*CB*

Crocus tommasinianus
TOMMIES

Crocuses, the harbingers of spring, afford the gardener some 80 species from which to choose. Most grow fairly easily, and with careful selection they supply bursts of color from late winter through spring. Chalice- or cup-shaped blooms open in the warmth of the sun to reveal three stamens. The small, grasslike foliage of winter- and spring-blooming crocuses emerges just before or as the flowers appear and continues growing until flowering has finished. In all species, a narrow white stripe runs down the center of each leaf. Spring-blooming crocuses are available in a wide

With careful selection, crocuses supply color from late winter through spring. Tommies are immune to the vagaries of winter weather and are among the first to bloom.

palette of colors including burnished gold, chrome-yellow, snow-white, ivory, royal-purple, violet, and lavender. Many species display bicolored or striped tepals. The soft lavender chalices of *Crocus tommasinianus* are a welcome sight in late winter and early spring, as this crocus is impervious to the vagaries of winter weather and is among the earliest to flower. It has petite, elegant blossoms of pale lavender with a silvery reverse and readily naturalizes without being aggressive.

NATIVE HABITAT The Balkans, Hungary, and Bulgaria

HARDINESS ZONES 3 to 8

HOW TO GROW Heavy, water-retentive, clay soils are inhospitable to crocuses. They prefer average, well-drained soil that contains sand or grit, full sun, and little or no water in summer. Spring-flowering crocuses do well under a canopy of deciduous trees and shrubs,

where they receive full sun while they are actively growing and the plants overhead haven't leafed out yet. Plant corms in the fall in groups or drifts for maximum visibility and impact, at a depth of 3 to 4 inches. *C. tommasinianus* and *C. biflorus* naturalize, and you can plant them in beds and borders as well as in lawn areas. Wait to mow until the crocus foliage has changed color and begins to die back. You can divide and move large clumps of crocuses while the foliage is still green or separate and replant offsets as corms go dormant.

CULTIVARS AND RELATED SPECIES *Crocus tommasinianus* 'Whitewell Purple' is a deep purple; 'Ruby Giant' is larger and more vigorous than the species. *C. ancyrensis,* the golden bunch crocus, sends up bright yellow-gold chalices and is very free-flowering. *C.cartwrightianus* 'Blue Bird' is creamy-white on the inside and lavender-blue on the outside. Bright, melon-colored stamens contrast with the soft buttermilk-yellow tepals of 'Cream Beauty', which is a darker color on the reverse. 'Ladykiller' sports glacier-white stripes on a purple background and stands out in the garden; 'Snow Bunting' has lavender stippling on white. *C. chrysanthus,* an early-blooming species with yellow flowers, is a parent of many of the early-blooming hybrids known as snow crocus. *C. sieberi* 'Tricolor' is easily recognized by its rich golden throat, ringed in white with purple. *C. vernus* is part of the lineage of plants that have come to be known as Dutch hybrid or large-flowering crocus. 'Jeanne d'Arc' shows off icy-white flowers contrasted with a deep purple base; 'Pickwick' has white and purple stripes. Hybrids of *C. vernus* are vigorous, long-lived, and appropriate for naturalizing. All are hardy in Zones 3 to 8.

COMPANION PLANTS Place crocuses near the front in perennial and mixed borders where they are easy to see. Their size makes them perfect for

rock gardens, and they can be layered in containers with daffodils (*Narcissus*), tulips, and grape hyacinths (*Muscari*), helping to provide a long season of bloom. *C. tommasinianus* is lovely massed underneath the overhanging branches of a winter-blooming witch-hazel (*Hamamelis*) or forming a skirt around *Mahonia* × *media* 'Charity'. Sunshine-yellow crocuses are pretty lighting up the ground beneath the arching stems of winter-white *Helleborus* × *hybridus*.   —LH

Cyclamen coum
WINTER CYCLAMEN, HARDY CYCLAMEN

The five swept-back petals of the squat pink flowers of winter cyclamen open from beaklike buds in the face of winter's chilly winds, keeping company with snowdrops (*Galanthus*) and a few optimistic daffodils (*Narcissus*) getting a jump on spring. Lovely heart-shaped leaves, often ringed with silver or gray, arise in autumn from flattened, circular tubers. Flower color varies from deep rosy-red to pure white. Leaf mottling is also variable, with pure silver- or pewter-colored leaves now being offered by specialty nurseries.

NATIVE HABITAT Open, rocky woods and scrub in Turkey

HARDINESS ZONES 6 (with protection) to 9

HOW TO GROW Give cyclamen moist humus-rich or loamy soil in light to partial shade. Plants emerge in autumn, so if you plan to mulch your beds, add the mulch before the leaves emerge so they can grow up through it and won't get buried. Deep mulch

Plant winter cyclamens in a shady spot and give them plenty of room to spread.

Site heath-spotted orchids carefully, as they dislike having their roots disturbed.

may smother plants and keep them from reseeding. Do not crowd winter cyclamen with aggressive perennials, and give them plenty of room to spread. With a rich pocket of soil for the roots, plants will grow well even among the shallow roots of mature trees. Plants self-sow freely where they are happy, and seedlings vary in leaf mottling and flower color, over time creating a decorative crazy quilt of variation.

CULTIVARS AND RELATED SPECIES
Winter cyclamens are sometimes sold by flower color or degree of silver in the leaves, but named selections are few and hard to find. *Cyclamen repandum* is a handsome species with mottled, arrow-shaped leaves and deep pink to white flowers with narrow, pointed petals. Plants are less hardy, so choose a protected spot. Position them where they will not be swamped by other plants. Zones 7 to 8.

COMPANION PLANTS Snowdrops (*Galanthus*) and cyclamen seem made for each other. They both scoff at winter with their delicate flowers. Plant them among early perennials such as Lenten roses (*Helleborus × hybridus*), lungwort (*Pulmonaria*) and under early shrubs like daphne, witch-hazel (*Hamamelis*) and wintersweet (*Chimonanthus praecox*).   —CB

Dactylorhiza maculata
HEATH-SPOTTED ORCHID
These exquisite, hardy terrestrial orchids produce captivating, dramatic flowers in shades of white, pink, lilac, purple, and red. The 30 species comprising this genus get their name from the Greek words "daktylos," for finger, which refers to the digitlike flattened tubers, and "rhiza," root. Fleshy, mid-green leaves are lancelike and often spotted in brown or purplish tones. Flowers are borne in dense,

upright racemes on 12- to 15-inch stems in late spring and early summer. Each flower has a protruding lower lip much like snapdragon (*Antirrhinum*).

NATIVE HABITAT Meadows, heaths, and marshy streamside areas in Europe, North Africa, and Asia; there is one North American species

HARDINESS ZONES 5 to 8

HOW TO GROW Heath-spotted orchids grow best in areas with cool summers, such as the Pacific Northwest and parts of the Northeast. They prefer the protective canopy of trees and woodland shrubs where they get partial shade and are shielded from the burning rays of the sun. These bulbs require moist, well-drained soil that has been amended with humus and leaf mold to a depth of 12 to 18 inches, but they won't tolerate immersion in standing water. They can be difficult to establish and dislike having their roots disturbed, since the tubers are viable for only a year. New tubers develop on the fingerlike appendages of the old roots.

CULTIVARS AND RELATED SPECIES *Dactylorhiza elata* is well adapted to garden use. Deep lilac-purple flower spikes rise above solid green leaves in June. You can site this species at the edge of a pond or in a woodland understory. Zones 6 to 8. *D. fuchsii* tolerates full sun if the soil is constantly damp. Green leaves overlaid with a dusting of silver offset baby-pink flowers with magenta splotches, which appear in June. Zones 5 to 8. *D. maculata* holds its vivid violet-purple bloom spikes above silvery-green-spotted leaves that enhance the flower color. Zones 5 to 8.

COMPANION PLANTS The upright flower spikes of *Dactylorhiza* species contrast beautifully with the colorful whorls of Japanese primrose (*Primula japonica*) and the rosette-shaped flowers of the candelabra primrose (*P. pulverulenta*). The lacy, creamy-white plumes of *Astilbe* 'Bridal Veil' make a soft, hazy background for the stiff, vertical forms of *Dactylorhiza* flowers.   —*LH*

Dicentra cucullaria
DUTCHMAN'S BREECHES
The curious flowers of Dutchman's breeches dangle on delicate arching stems and look to some like inverted pantaloons hung out to dry. To my eye, they look more like molars pulled out, roots and all. However you describe them, these early, fragrant flowers above intricately dissected, gray-green leaves are sure to please. Plants grow from clustered yellow tubers that look like corn kernels.

NATIVE HABITAT Woodlands and floodplain forests throughout eastern and central North America

HARDINESS ZONES 3 to 8

HOW TO GROW Plant the fragile clusters of tubers 2 to 3 inches deep in rich, evenly moist soil in a spot with plenty of spring sun. The plants take several years to settle in, and blooms may be sparse until they are well established. Self-sown seedlings may be plentiful, but they take several years to reach flowering size. Plants go dormant by late spring.

CULTIVARS AND RELATED SPECIES *Dicentra canadensis*, squirrel corn, has heart-shaped flowers with a delicious scent reminiscent of hyacinth. The flowers are densely crowded on short stems above ferny, gray-green leaves. Zones 4 to 8.

COMPANION PLANTS Dutchman's

North American native Dutchman's breeches take several years to settle in, and blooms may be sparse at first.

NATIVE HABITAT Rich deciduous woods, dry rocky woods, savannas, and prairies from Maryland and Minnesota south to Georgia and Texas

HARDINESS ZONES 4 to 8

HOW TO GROW Plant shooting stars in moist, humus-rich soil in sun or shade. Once plants are dormant, the soil can become dry and the site quite shady. They prefer neutral or slightly acidic soil. Divide multicrowned clumps in summer or fall and replant the individual crowns with the roots spread evenly in a circle.

CULTIVARS AND RELATED SPECIES *Dodecatheon meadia* forma *album* is white-flowered. 'Comet' is rich pink. 'Queen Victoria' is a 10- to 12-inch plant with deep rose-purple flowers. All are hardy in Zones 4 to 8. *D. pulchellum*, beautiful shooting star, includes plants that were formerly classified as *D. amethystinum*. This species is more delicate, with 10-inch oval to spatula-shaped leaves and rose-pink to deep magenta flowers. Plants are quite variable in size, from 3 to 20 inches tall depending on geographic location and position. They require limey soil in full sun or partial shade. Zones 4 to 7.

COMPANION PLANTS Shooting stars give wings to the spring garden. Plant drifts among decorative groundcovers such as wild ginger (*Asarum*), Jacob's ladder (*Polemonium reptans*), North American native cranesbill (*Geranium maculatum*), and ferns that will hide the spaces left during dormancy. In prairie gardens or rockeries, plant them with pinks (*Dianthus*), sand phlox (*Phlox bifida*), prairie phlox (*Phlox pilosa*), and golden Alexanders (*Zizia*). —CB

breeches spread a delicate carpet through which ferns, wake robins (*Trillium*), and other bulbs can easily pass, making a beautifully layered spring scene. Hellebores, hostas, and species peonies (*Paeonia*) are good companions with persistent leaves. —CB

Dodecatheon meadia
SHOOTING STAR

The curious, fragrant flowers of shooting stars are like darts with swirling streamers. These delicate, ephemeral plants present basal rosettes of oval to broadly lance-shaped foliage that disappear after flowering. Naked flower spikes 1 to 2 feet tall sport a regal crown of gracefully arching 1-inch pink or white flowers. Fleshy white roots radiate in a circle from the crown.

Winter aconite self-sows to form dense colonies over time.

Eranthis hyemalis
WINTER ACONITE

The cheery, upward-facing buttercup-yellow flowers of winter aconite add a splash of sunshine to the early-spring garden. Each single flower is surrounded by a collar of dissected leaves with narrow segments on succulent stems 1 to 4 inches tall. Plants grow from small tuberous roots.

NATIVE HABITAT Open woods of southern to eastern Europe; naturalized throughout Europe

HARDINESS ZONES 4 to 8

HOW TO GROW Plant in rich humusy or loamy soil in a spot with plenty of spring sun. Soak the tubers overnight in warm water before planting, and set them 1 to 2 inches below the soil level. Plants will self-sow to form large, showy colonies that become quite congested over time. Transplant "in the green," which is to say just after flowering, or wait until the leaves are yellowing off. Sometimes winter aconite is collected from the wild. For more information on the problems of wild collection and what to look for when purchasing bulbs, see "Buyer Beware," on page 14.

CULTIVARS AND RELATED SPECIES *Eranthis cilicia* has larger flowers in proportion to the leaves, which have very thin, spidery segments that emerge tinged with bronze, creating a showy effect with orange primroses (*Primula*). Zones 4 to 8. *E. stellata* is a handsome species with deeply dissected leaves and open, white flowers with blue stamens. It is finally becoming more available. Zones 4 to 8.

COMPANION PLANTS Snowdrops (*Galanthus*), cyclamens, and other early bloomers are good companions, intermingled with hellebores, primroses (*Primula*), and ferns. Use a generous planting under winter-blooming shrubs such as white forsythia (*Abeliophyllum distichum*), daphnes, and *Viburnum × bodnantense* 'Dawn'.—CB

Eremurus stenophyllus
FOXTAIL LILY, KING'S SPEAR, DESERT CANDLE

Few plants are as dramatic in bloom or as sought after for cut flowers as foxtail lilies. Planted in drifts at the back or middle of the border, the tall candles of bloom create bold, vertical accents. Hundreds of small, starry flowers exhibiting showy stamens are borne on a single stalk. As the flowers fade, the straplike foliage begins to die back and wither, so plant foxtail lilies among perennials that will hide the void when they go dormant in mid-summer. In spring the foliage is susceptible to slug damage. Long, brittle, fleshy, finger-shaped roots extend out from a rhizome, making foxtail lilies difficult to transplant and divide. *Eremurus stenophyllus* is the shortest of the genus, bearing a 3-foot-tall spire of gleaming yellow flowers.

NATIVE HABITAT Dry grassland, semi-desert, and mountain slopes in western and central Asia in areas with long, hot summers, fall rains, and cool winters

HARDINESS ZONES 5 to 8

HOW TO GROW Choose a site for foxtail lilies carefully. They need full sun with rich, well-drained soil and don't tolerate heavy, clayey soils. You can plant rhizomes in the fall or set out plants grown in 1- to 2-gallon containers in late spring. Cultivate the soil to a depth of 2 feet, adding organic matter. Dig a hole that's about 8 inches deep and wide enough to accommo-date the radiating roots, spread a 2- to 3-inch layer of fine gravel or chicken grit in the bottom of the hole, arrange the roots on top, and backfill carefully since the roots are brittle and easily broken. Plants break dormancy early in spring and may be protected from late-spring frost damage by a blanket of mulch. Propagate plants from divisions after three to four years by lifting and separating the crowns.

CULTIVARS AND RELATED SPECIES *Eremurus stenophyllus* subsp. *stenophyllus* (syn. *E. bungei*) showcases its egg-yolk-yellow flowers on 5-foot stalks. *E. × isabellinus* (sometimes listed as Shelford hybrids, a crossing of *E. stenopyllus* and *E. olgae*) are garden-worthy hybrids and include *E.* 'Isobel', which produces lovely coral-pink flowers on 5- to 6-foot stems. *E.* 'Rosalind' sports blooms of bright pink. All are hardy in Zones 5 to 8.

COMPANION PLANTS Foxtail lilies play a starring role in the summer border when paired with the fire-engine-red clusters of Maltese cross *(Lychnis chalcedonica)*, the flat-topped, lemon-yellow inflorescenses of *Achillea* 'Moonshine', and the floating, silver-blue globes of *Echinops* 'Taplow Blue'. Salvias, catmint (*Nepeta*), lavenders, and cranesbills (*Geranium*)—good knitters and weavers—are excellent infill as the foxtail lilies go dormant.   —*LH*

Erythronium revolutum
COAST FAWN LILY, TROUT LILY, DOG-TOOTH VIOLET

Coast fawn lily gets its name from the mottled leaves that resemble a speckled fawn. This is a showy member of a large genus of delicate spring wildflowers with paired green or mottled leaves and single to triple nodding flowers with reflexed (curved backward) petals and sepals and protruding stamens. This species sports pink flowers on 8- to 10-inch stems and mottled leaves. Plants go dormant immediately after flowering.

NATIVE HABITAT Open woods and scrubby meadows in the coastal range of Oregon and Washington

HARDINESS ZONES 4 to 8

HOW TO GROW Plant coast fawn lily corms as soon as they are available in fall in moist, humus-rich soil. Spring sun is essential, but once the plants are dormant, the site can become quite shady. Take care not to dig into the clumps during the dormant season. Self-sown seedlings will appear, but they develop slowly and may take three to five years to bloom.

CULTIVARS AND RELATED SPECIES A number of hybrid selections are available. *Erythronium* 'Kondo' has three to five yellow flowers with a brown basal ring above weakly mottled leaves that fade to green. 'Pagoda' has one to three clear yellow flowers and mottled leaves. 'White Beauty' has creamy-white flowers with a brown

ring at the throat on compact stems to 6 inches tall. All are hardy in Zones 4 to 7. *E. albidum,* white trout lily, is a diminutive species 4 to 8 inches tall with white flowers sporting a purple or blue blush on the outside of the sepals. The paired leaves are heavily mottled. Zones 4 to 8. *E. americanum,* yellow trout lily, is a yellow-flowered species with heavily mottled foliage. Zones 3 to 8. Both are native to eastern North America. *E. dens-canis,* European dog-tooth violet, is a squat, floriferous plant with rose-pink to deep lilac flowers and mottled oval leaves. 'Lilac Wonder' with pale purple flowers and 'Rose Queen' with deep pink flowers, are two of many named selections. Zones 2 to 7. *E. grandiflorum,* avalanche-lily, is native to western North America and has one to three bright yellow flowers on slender stalks 6 to 18 inches tall above green leaves. Plants dislike heat and may be difficult to grow in the East. Zones 3 to 7. *E. tuolumnense* is a tall, yellow-flowered species with plain green leaves. It's native to California. Zones 4 to 7.

COMPANION PLANTS Plant the graceful trout lilies in drifts with spring bulbs, wildflowers, and early perennials. Combine them with leafy plants like lungwort (*Pulmonaria*), wild bleeding heart (*Dicentra eximia*), ferns, and hostas to cover the gaps left in summer when plants are dormant.   —*CB*

Fritillaria imperialis
CROWN IMPERIAL
The largest and showiest of its genus, crown imperial produces 2- to 4-foot stems, which emerge from a whorl of shiny green foliage and are topped by clusters of downward-facing umbels of

The nodding flowers of coast fawn lily rise above the blooms of wood anemone.

Plant crown imperials as soon as you purchase them, as the fleshy bulbs dry out fast.

red, orange, or yellow crowned by a topknot of small leaves. By far the best known of the fritillaries, *F. imperialis* was also the first to be cultivated; it was introduced by Clusius in the 16th century. When touched or crushed, both the bulbs and foliage exude an odor redolent of skunk, which some may find offensive. The genus encompasses some 100 species that range in size from diminutive rock-garden denizens to showy border beauties. Some species thrive in full sun while others come from damp meadows. All have cup- or bell-shaped, pendulous flowers that, depending on the species, are checkered or blotched with shades of green, white, or purple-brown. This bicolored, patterned effect is reflected in the genus name, which is derived from "fritillas," meaning dice box.

NATIVE HABITAT Northern Hemisphere, Mediterranean, North America, and Asia

HARDINESS ZONES 4 to 9, depending on the species

HOW TO GROW Most fritillaries perform well in full sun or light shade in moist, well-drained soil that has been amended with organic matter. Plant bulbs as soon as you purchase them, as they dry out quickly and are not viable once dry. Set them at a depth of four times the height of the bulb. Some species, including *F. imperialis* and *F. persica,* have open-crowned bulbs that can rot once planted. Line the planting hole with several inches of chicken grit or builders' sand to create better drainage, and place bulbs on their sides to keep water from collecting in their crowns. For maximum impact, space larger species 12 to 18 inches apart and smaller species 4 to 6 inches apart. Species that require dry soil when dormant are good candidates for alpine gardens and containers.

CULTIVARS AND RELATED SPECIES Cultivars of *Fritillaria imperialis* include 'Lutea Maxima', which bears brilliant yellow flowers, and 'Rubra Maxima', a deep vermilion-red.

F. meleagris, the snake's-head fritillary or Guinea-hen flower, grows in moist conditions in full sun or partial shade. The petite, checkered purple flowers are borne on 8- to 10-inch stems in mid-spring. 'Alba' has snow-white flowers and can be more difficult to find. The slate-purple pendant bells of *F. persica* are displayed on 2-foot stems and are hardiest in fast-draining soils.

COMPANION PLANTS The red-orange foliage and carrot-orange bracts of *Euphorbia* 'Dixter' and the upward-facing, deep purple chalices of *Tulipa* 'Negrita' stop traffic when partnered with *F. imperalis* 'Rubra Maxima'. Shades of pink and purple tulips harmonize with the dusky purple bells and silvery foliage sheen of *F. persica*. White-blooming *Helleborus* × *hybridus* and the two-toned mahogany and gold flowers of *Primula* Gold Laced Group are an interesting foil for the checkered purple nodding heads of *F. meleagris*.   —*LH*

Galanthus nivalis
COMMON SNOWDROP

Snowdrops are among the most popular bulbs, beloved more for their early flowering than for arresting color or large flower size. The diminutive plants have two to three strappy leaves around a slender stalk bearing a single nodding, often fragrant flower with three floppy outer sepals and three overlapping inner segments stained with green. Plants grow from true bulbs. Hundreds of selections of this and other species are available. Collectors will pay outrageous prices for new introductions.

NATIVE HABITAT Woodlands, shaded ravines, and bottomlands from central Europe to Turkey

HARDINESS ZONES 3 to 8

HOW TO GROW Plant snowdrops in humus-rich, evenly moist soil with plenty of winter and early-spring sun. Soak dormant bulbs overnight in warm water to increase their chances of survival. Bulbs stored dry over the summer are often desiccated and slow to recover. For this reason, the practice of transplanting snowdrops in the green (just after flowering while still actively growing) was started. This method can be effective, but bulbs must be replanted immediately. If they're dug as the leaves are fading, success is also assured, with less stress to the bulb.

CULTIVARS AND RELATED SPECIES *Galanthus nivalis* 'Atkinsii', a hybrid, has erect flower stalks and flowers nearly an inch long. 'Flore Pleno' has fully double flowers with frilly centers surrounded by three sepals. 'Magnet' has large flowers borne on slender, arching pedicels. 'S. Arnott' (also sold

Soaking the bulbs of common snowdrops before planting increases their chances of success.

as 'Sam Arnott') is a robust selection 6 to 8 inches tall with large, showy flowers held on erect stalks above the leaves. 'Viridapices' sports a green signal on each of the outer sepals. All are hardy in Zones 3 to 8. *G. elwesii,* giant snowdrop, has wide, upright gray-green leaves and large flowers with rounded sepals around inner segments that are green at both the tip and the base. Zones 4 to 8. Due to extensive wild collection, giant snowdrops as well as some other snowdrop species are in danger of vanishing in their native habitats. For more information on the problems of wild collection and what to look for when purchasing bulbs, see "Buyer Beware," page 14. *G. ikariae* has wide green leaves and smallish flowers with green-edged inner segments. Zones 4 to 8. *G. plicatus* is a robust species with gray-green leaves folded backward around the edges. Showy white flowers have long sepals. *G. plicatus* subsp. *byzantinus* has greener leaves and apical as well as basal flairs on the inner flower segments. Zones 3 to 8.

COMPANION PLANTS Plant drifts of snowdrops among early plants such as hellebores, combined with other bulbs such as cyclamens and fume root (*Corydalis solida*). Ferns, phlox, blue-eyed Mary (*Omphalodes*) and barrenwort (*Epimedium*) are excellent companions. —*CB*

Hermodactylus tuberosus
WIDOW IRIS, SNAKES-HEAD IRIS
The fragrant but somberly colored iris-like flowers of widow iris seem draped in a mourning shroud. The standards are dusky yellow and the falls are nearly black. The widow iris is closely related to true iris; the only botanical difference is that it has a single locule

Widow iris produces foliage in fall and blooms in spring.

in the ovary rather than three. Plants grow from tubers and spread to form large colonies.

NATIVE HABITAT Scrub and rocky Mediterranean meadows from France east to Turkey and Israel

HARDINESS ZONES 6 to 8

HOW TO GROW Plant in humus-rich, evenly moist soil in full sun or light shade. Widow iris needs a good baking while dormant in summer. Plants produce foliage in autumn and bloom in spring, so make sure the soil is moist when the plants are in active growth.

CULTIVARS AND RELATED SPECIES *Iris bucharica* is one of several species known as the Juno iris. These natives of the eastern Mediterranean and Turkey grow from true bulbs with thick, fleshy roots and produce leafy stalks that look like delicate corn plants crowned with axillary clusters of fragrant yellow flowers with creamy-white standards. *I. caucasica* and *I. magnifica,* both white-flowered, are sometimes available from specialty nurseries. Zones 3 to 9.

COMPANION PLANTS Species tulips and other plants adapted to dry summers, such as catmints (*Nepeta*), calamints (*Calamintha*), pinks (*Dianthus*), and beard-tongues (*Penstemon*) are good companions for clumps of widow iris.   —*CB*

Hyacinthoides hispanica
SPANISH BLUEBELL

Bluebells colonize woods and meadows in their native habitats, are vigorous garden growers, and easily naturalize in grass or in a wild or woodland garden. Spanish bluebells form large clumps of lance-shaped, basal leaves from which flower stalks with 6 to 15 lavender-blue bells emerge. The bulbs are difficult to eradicate once established and can easily overtake less robust plants. Many gardeners report that touching the bulb, stems, leaves, or flowers causes skin irritation. *Hyacinthoides* species are closely related to *Scilla*.

NATIVE HABITAT Deciduous woodlands and moist meadows in western Europe and North Africa

Spanish bluebells easily naturalize in grass or in a wild or woodland garden.

HARDINESS ZONES 4 to 9

HOW TO GROW This easy-to-grow genus prefers a site in dappled to part shade with average, moist, well-drained acidic soil—for example, under the canopy of deciduous trees where they are exposed to the sun's rays in the spring. With adequate moisture, bluebells also do well in full sun. Plant bulbs 3 inches deep in fall or divide and transplant established clumps after they bloom.

CULTIVARS AND RELATED SPECIES *Hyacynthoides hispanica* 'Excelsior' has lavender-blue flowers striped with blue and 'Rosabella' is a soft rosy-violet. *H. non-scripta,* English bluebells, were previously known as *Endymion non-scripta, Scilla non-scripta,* and *S. nutans.* Fragrant, lavender-blue flowers with tepals that curve at the tip are arrayed in one-sided racemes. The bulbs are poisonous, and in times past their viscous juice was used as a starch and for bookbinding.

COMPANION PLANTS Bluebells can be used as a groundcover in shrub borders and under trees.   —*LH*

Hyacinthus orientalis
DUTCH HYACINTH

In full bloom, Dutch hyacinth cultivars have the power to overcome the senses. It is impossible to ignore the sturdy 8-inch flower stalks covered by up to 40 tubular flared bells in an array of vivid hues from white through pink, yellow, purple, and blue. The flower heads exude a heady, spicy fragrance redolent of jasmine. *Hyacinthus orientalis,* the species that gave rise to the nearly 200 selections available today, is

First cultivated in Holland more than 400 years ago, Dutch hyacinths continue to be popular, with close to 200 selections available today. Above is 'Gipsy Queen'.

much more refined and natural-looking, with elegant, winsome flower spikes carrying far fewer bells than its exhibitionist siblings. Hyacinths were first cultivated in Holland more than 400 years ago. The Dutch speculated in hyacinth bulbs in the 17th and 18th centuries. Ingesting any part of the plant causes stomach upsets, and touching the bulbs or foliage may exacerbate skin allergies.

NATIVE HABITAT Western and central Asia

HARDINESS ZONES 5 to 9

HOW TO GROW Plant Dutch hyacinths 5 inches deep in warm areas and 6 to 8 inches deep in northern gardens, in rich, well-drained soil in full sun or partial shade. Plants will produce larger blooms in the first season and diminish in size thereafter. An organic mulch, applied in successive springs when the basal foliage appears, can help maintain flower size. Another option is to dig up the bulbs and transplant them to a woodland or less formal area of the garden after the first season.

CULTIVARS AND RELATED SPECIES
Hyacinthus orientalis 'Delft Blue', with pale blue-lavender blooms, is easy to force. 'City of Haarlem' is an old favorite dating back to 1898, known for its pale butter-yellow bells that fade to ivory. 'Gipsy Queen' is an unusual shade of coral-peach that consorts well with blue or purple hyacinths and cream daffodils. 'Pink Festival' is a multistemmed cultivar with pale pink flowers; it is easily forced. All are hardy in Zones 5 to 9.

COMPANION PLANTS Use in large drifts in beds or place bulbs in groups of 6 to 12 near the edges of annual bulb displays or in perennial or mixed borders. You can force *H. orientalis* cultivars indoors or plant them in containers for display in entryways and on terraces and patios. —*LH*

Spring starflower stays in bloom for a month or more beginning in late winter.

Ipheion uniflorum
SPRING STARFLOWER

The starry, sweet-scented blue flowers open en masse on sunny days, all pointing toward the light and thus presenting an enthusiastic show. Plants produce straplike sea-green leaves from true bulbs that increase rapidly to form dense, floriferous clumps. This onion relative reveals its kinship by the odor it exudes when foliage or bulbs are damaged.

NATIVE HABITAT Scrub, open meadows, and swales in Argentina and Uruguay

HARDINESS ZONES 4 to 9

HOW TO GROW Plant in average to rich, humusy or loamy soil in full sun to partial shade. New leaves are produced in late autumn, and plants begin flowering in late winter, with the show gaining momentum in early spring. After a month or more of bloom, the plants go dormant and can tolerate very dry conditions.

CULTIVARS AND RELATED SPECIES
Ipheion uniflorum 'Froyle Mill' has gorgeous purple flowers. *I. dialystemon* 'Rolf Fiedler' is an excellent selection with deep blue, fat flowers. 'Wisley Blue' is a prolific spreader with medium blue flowers and narrow leaves. Self-sown seedlings are plentiful, and color varies in the offspring of any named selection.

COMPANION PLANTS Spring starflower really shines planted en masse as a groundcover under shrubs and flowering trees or in drifts among late-emerging plants such as peonies (*Paeonia*) and hostas. Use them in a rock garden or plant them atop a rock wall, where they may seed into the crevices to enchanting effect.   —*CB*

Iris reticulata
RETICULATED IRIS, DWARF IRIS

For a blast of rich color in early spring, you can't beat the reticulated iris. Though the flowers fade in just a few days, the early color is worth the ephemeral joy they bring. After the fragrant blue to purple flowers fade, the cylindrical leaves elongate to a foot or more until the plant goes dormant in summer. Plants grow from a true bulb with a papery tunic.

NATIVE HABITAT Scrub and open, rocky meadows of Turkey

HARDINESS ZONES 4 to 9

HOW TO GROW Plant reticulated irises in rich, moist but well-drained soil in full sun or light shade. Before planting soak the bulbs overnight For best bloom plants need a good baking in summer. In many areas of the country, the bulbous species are best grown as short-lived perennials because they do not rebloom well.

CULTIVARS AND RELATED SPECIES *Iris reticulata* 'Cantab' has pale blue flowers. 'Harmony' has royal-blue flowers. 'Joyce' has sky-blue flowers. 'J.S. Dijt' has red-violet flowers. 'Pixie' is the deepest indigo, with near-black falls. *I. histrioides,* harput iris, is another early-spring bulbous species similar to *I. reticulata,* with bright purple-blue flowers. 'Frank Elder' is a hybrid with unusually attractive pale blue flowers. 'George' is a popular hybrid selection with violet-purple flowers. 'Katherine Hodgkin' has yellow and blue mottled flowers that are hard to describe but lovely to behold. 'Major' has deep blue flowers. All are hardy in Zones 4 to 9. *I. xiphium,* Spanish iris or poor man's orchid, is a delicate species that opens its yellow or purple flowers in spring atop 18-inch stems. This species has been extensively hybridized with the early-summer blooming *I. latifolia* (formerly *I. xiphioides*), English iris, to produce the popular hybrids known as "Dutch iris." Both species are attrac-

tive in their own right, but most gardeners grow the readily available and flamboyant Dutch hybrids. Dozens of named selections are available. Zones 4 to 8. *I. danfordiae,* Danford iris, has flattened, bright yellow flowers that emerge in early spring before the leaves. The curled, cylindrical leaves elongate to 12 inches immediately after flowering and disappear by sum-

Reticulated iris fades in a few days but provides welcome splashes of early color.

mer. Dry soil is imperative for this species to make an appearance the second year after planting. Zones 5 to 8.

COMPANION PLANTS Plant this small bulbous iris in a rock garden or at the front of a border with spring bulbs and mounding or mat-forming plants such as moss phlox (*Phlox subulata*), thyme, and rock cress (*Arabis* and *Aubrieta*) for contrast. —*CB*

Ixiolirion tataricum
SIBERIAN LILY

This taxonomically confusing plant has been jostled around more than a commuter on the New York subway. Though relatively unknown to most gardeners, it is an attractive bulb deserving of wider popularity. Umbels of starry, upward-facing purple-blue flowers open in late spring and early summer above wispy, grasslike foliage.

NATIVE HABITAT Open, rocky slopes and scrub from Turkey and North Africa east to Siberia

HARDINESS ZONES 6 to 9

HOW TO GROW Set these true bulbs in a spot with rich, evenly moist soil in full sun or light shade. Plants need a good summer baking in a well-drained spot and will rot with too much summer moisture.

COMPANION PLANTS Combine Siberian lily with dryland or Mediterranean plants such as yuccas and lavenders, as well as sand phlox (*Phlox bifida*), catmints (*Nepeta*), beard-tongues (*Penstemon*), and yarrows (*Achillea*). Tulips, *Calochortus,* and *Triteleia* share the need for dry summers, making them excellent companions. Huge-flowered hybrid tulips would obscure the subtle beauty of this bulb, so choose delicate species as companions.   —*CB*

Leucojum vernum
SPRING SNOWFLAKE

The chunky fragrant flowers of spring snowflake look like white Victorian lampshades decorated with drooping emerald tassels. The buds emerge just ahead of or with the foliage, which expands to 6 inches as the flowers mature. The single or twin bell-shaped flowers have six fused tepals with pointed tips, each marked by a green flair. Plants grow from a true bulb.

NATIVE HABITAT Woodlands and ravines throughout central Europe

HARDINESS ZONES 4 to 8

HOW TO GROW Plant in moist, humus-rich soil in full to partial sun. Before planting soak the white bulbs overnight in warm water to rehydrate them. If stored too long, bulbs may become moldy or so desiccated that they do not grow. Order early and plant the bulbs as soon as they arrive. This species can be moved in the green (just after flowering) or as the leaves are yellowing.

CULTIVARS AND RELATED SPECIES *Leucojum vernum* var. *carpathicum* has yellow rather than green tips. For generations, *L. aestivum,* summer snowflake, has been passed around southern gardens, where it blooms in

Siberian lily will rot if it gets too much moisture after going dormant in summer.

The fragrant flowers of spring snowflake nod above winter aconite.

early to mid-spring, not summer. Farther north, the four to six nodding white chalices with deep green flairs open in succession atop stems to 2 feet tall in late spring. Plants tolerate moist to wet soil and often grow in areas inundated by floodwater. 'Gravetye Giant' is a particularly robust and floriferous selection to 2 feet tall. Hardy in Zones 4 to 9.

COMPANION PLANTS I use drifts of this charming and showy bulb with hellebores and ferns as well as other early bulbs. The flowers are an inch across and show up better than the more delicate snowdrops, making a good show under shrubs and trees that are at some distance from the path.   —*CB*

Mertensia virginica
VIRGINIA BLUEBELL
Bluebells are one of the few plants that actually bring the blue of the sky down to earth. These ephemeral spring wildflowers adorn the garden with nodding clusters of sky-blue bell-shaped flowers on delicate stems to 2 feet tall. Plants produce succulent blue-green basal foliage rosettes from stout, thickened tuberous roots. The leaves die down as soon as flowering is complete.

NATIVE HABITAT Moist deciduous woods, floodplains, streamsides and clearings from New York and Minnesota south to Kansas and Alabama

HARDINESS ZONES 3 to 9

HOW TO GROW Plant bluebells in consistently moist, well-drained humus-rich soil in sun or shade. Deep purple shoots emerge in early spring and quickly expand to reveal the buds. The flowers begin opening as the stems elongate. Take care not to dig into the dormant clumps by accident. Self-sown seedlings will bloom the second or third year.

CULTIVARS AND RELATED SPECIES
Mertensia virginica 'Alba' has white flowers. Plants with pink and lavender flowers are occasionally found in the wild and in gardens, but no named selections are available. *M. paniculata,* tall lungwort, is a succulent plant from western North America with upright stems from 2 to 3 feet tall sporting thin, quilted oval blue-green leaves with pointed tips. The half-inch nodding flowers open in late spring and early summer. Zones 4 to 7.

COMPANION PLANTS Bluebells are among the few native wildflowers that have been grown here and abroad since colonial times. They are lovely in a shaded garden in the company of spring bulbs such as daffodils (*Narcissus*) and species tulips. Plant

The foliage of ephemeral Virginia bluebells vanishes soon after the plants flower.

them in a carpet of wood anemone (*Anemone nemorosa*) punctuated by wake robins (*Trillium*), shooting star (*Dodecatheon*), woodland phlox (*Phlox divaricata*), and ferns. Combinations should include a few plants with persistent foliage such as wild ginger (*Asarum*) and barrenwort (*Epimedium*) to fill the gaps left when the ephemeral plants go dormant.   —*CB*

Muscari armeniacum
GRAPE HYACINTH

Grape hyacinths are often found naturalized underneath trees and shrubs in old gardens where their cobalt-blue cones of tiny, grape- or urn-shaped flowers are a source of nectar for bees from early to mid-spring. In all of the 30 species in the genus, narrow, linear leaves appear in fall and begin to wither and die back after flowering. Different species bloom in shades of lavender, purple-blue, white, and pale blue. Flowers vary in shape and may face upward or downward. In most species

the mouth of the flower is constricted, which helps to distinguish them from their kissing cousins, the *Hyacinthus* species, which have open mouths.

NATIVE HABITAT Mediterranean and southwest Asia

HARDINESS ZONES 4 to 8

HOW TO GROW Plant bulbs in autumn 3 to 4 inches deep in full sun or light shade in rich, well-drained soil. All species bloom in the spring and are summer-dormant and therefore may be planted underneath trees and spring-blooming shrubs as long as they receive full sun before the plants overhead leaf out. Divide grape hyacinths when their leaves turn yellow. *Muscari armeniacum* and *M. botryoides* are vigorous self-sowers and can, in optimum conditions, be rather aggressive; *M. botryoides* is turning up on some regional invasive-species watch lists. According to the Southeast Exotic Pest Plant Council, *M. botryoides* is

Grape hyacinth flowers are a source of nectar for bees from early to mid-spring.

considered invasive in Tennessee and should not be planted there.

CULTIVARS AND RELATED SPECIES
Muscari armeniacum 'Blue Spike' is a double form with long-lasting, deep blue flowers. 'Saphir' has deep blue flowers rimmed in white. 'Valerie Finnis' bears incredible light blue flowers, a color seldom seen in nature. *M. latifolium* has two-toned flowers: The uppermost sterile, round flowers are true blue, and the lower ones are violet-purple.

COMPANION PLANTS Grape hyacinths make an eye-catching carpet beneath early-blooming azaleas and rhododendrons. They are also attractive grown in clusters along the edges of walkways or scattered throughout a perennial bed. They thrive in containers where they may be mixed with crocuses, tulips, and daffodils (*Narcissus*) for a long-lasting display of color.—*LH*

Narcissus
HYBRID DAFFODILS
Some of the best known and most beloved of all spring-blooming bulbs, daffodils are easy to grow. They seldom need dividing, are virtually disease-free, and are unappealing to deer as well as mice and other rodents because all parts of the plant are toxic. Daffodils make long-lasting cut flowers, but they should be handled with care as the sap may cause skin irritations. Thousands of hybrid cultivars are available in a wide range of sizes, flower forms, and colors. Each flower is composed of a trumpet or cup called the corona, which is surrounded by six petals that form the perianth. Daffodils are organized into 13 divisions on the basis of their flower form. Yellow is the color most often associated with daffodils, but they also bloom in white, pink, and orange, and many are bicolored—that is to say, the corona and the perianth have different colors. Daffodils are usually described as early-, mid-, or late-blooming, and it is possible to have them in flower over a three-month period. Strap-shaped foliage appears in late winter.

NATIVE HABITAT Garden hybrids

HARDINESS ZONES 4 to 9

HOW TO GROW Daffodils require full sun or dappled shade in well-drained, neutral to acidic soil that has been amended with organic matter. In fall, plant bulbs 4 to 6 inches deep, depending on the size of the bulb. Space smaller-flowering bulbs 4 inches apart and those bearing larger blooms 8 to 12 inches apart. Allow foliage to ripen for 6 to 8 weeks before cutting or mowing, so that the bulbs can store food for next year's growth. Propagate by dividing clumps or removing offsets as clumps go dormant in summer.

CULTIVARS AND RELATED SPECIES
Narcissus 'Sir Winston Churchill', one of the best double forms, has creamy-white blooms with a gold center, stands 14 to 16 inches tall, and exudes a strong, sweet fragrance. 'Ice Follies', classified as a large-cupped narcissus, is a tried-and-true variety with white petals encircling a chartreuse-yellow crown on sturdy 16-inch stems. 'Minnow', a tazetta form, is an ivory and pale yellow miniature, bearing clusters of four to five flowers per stem. 'Waterperry' has a pale yellow corona splashed with apricot and an ivory perianth borne on 10- to 12-inch stems. 'Salome' is one of the so-called pink-flowered forms. The 18-inch stems exhibit a flower with an apricot-pink funnel set off by bright white petals.

COMPANION PLANTS Daffodils naturalize readily under deciduous trees and shrubs, as long as they have adequate sun in the spring while the bulbs are growing. Plant them in groups in all your perennial and mixed borders alongside peonies (*Paeonia*), wallflowers (*Erysimum*), euphorbias, campanulas, and rock cress (*Arabis* and *Aubrieta*). They also make good container plants, and some varieties can be forced indoors. —*LH*

Narcissus species
WILD JONQUIL, POLYANTHUS NARCISSUS
Species *Narcissus* are the ancestors of the many hybrids used in gardens the world over. Most are small in stature with delicate, simple flowers and have a place in the rock garden, alpine house, containers, and bulb frame. When compared with the size and form of many hybrids, the species appear more natural and elegant.

NATIVE HABITAT Spain, Turkey, North Africa, and Portugal

There are thousands of daffodil cultivars in a wide range of sizes, flower forms, and hues. Above is 'Ice Follies'.

Most wild jonquils, the ancestors of many modern hybrid daffodils, are small in stature with delicate little flowers.

HARDINESS ZONES 4 to 9

HOW TO GROW Species *Narcissus* have the same basic requirements as the hybrids (see above) although some may require special conditions to thrive.

CULTIVARS AND RELATED SPECIES The flowers of *Narcissus bulbocodium,* known as hoop petticoat daffodil, have a small perianth and open-faced funnels of soft yellow borne on 4- to 6-inch stems. They are good subjects for the rock garden, pot culture, or a cold greenhouse. *N. jonquilla* exudes a sweet, strong scent. The golden-yellow flowers, several to a stem, are held on 12-inch stems. *N. poeticus* has upward-facing flowers with a white perianth and yellow corona.

COMPANION PLANTS The more robust species can be planted out in the garden just like the hybrids. —*LH*

Nectaroscordum siculum subsp. *bulgaricum*
SICILIAN HONEY GARLIC
Nectaroscordum is a small genus that derives its name from *nectar,* "the drink of the gods," and *scordium,* which means "the plant smelling of garlic." When crushed, stem, leaf, and flower all exude the pungent scent of garlic. The nodding, bell-shaped flowers bloom in late spring in loose umbels atop 3-foot stems. The stunning pendant bells are creamy-white suffused with pink-purple and green and tinged with apple-green at the base. The grassy leaves appear in spring and disappear as the flowers fade. These plants are closely related to onions, *Allium,* and were at one time classified in the same genus.

NATIVE HABITAT Southern Europe and western Asia

HARDINESS ZONES 4 to 8

HOW TO GROW For best effect, plant honey garlic bulbs 2 inches deep and 12 to 18 inches apart in clusters of 3 to 5 in average, well-drained soil in full sun or partial shade. Place them among perennials or annuals so that the yellow, withering foliage is camouflaged as it dies back and disappears. Propagate by saving and planting seed, or dig up bulbs and separate offsets in early summer.

CULTIVARS AND RELATED SPECIES *Nectaroscordum siculum* is often sold as *N. siculum* subsp. *bulgaricum*. It would take a botanist to tell the difference, which is a slight variation in color.

COMPANION PLANTS Honey garlic plants take up very little space in the garden and are easy to use in a perennial or mixed border, where their height and interestingly shaped flowers add a touch of the exotic.

Displaying its unusual flowers atop yard-high stems, Sicilian honey garlic looks best when dotted among emerging perennials that will later hide the withering bulb foliage.

The muted colors of the flowers are intensified when seen against a backdrop of the dusky, mulberry-toned foliage of purple smoke tree (*Cotinus coggygria* 'Royal Purple'). They add a sense of verticality and interest when mixed with the rounded shape, wine-tinted foliage, and chartreuse bracts of *Euphorbia dulcis* 'Chameleon' and the ferny foliage and bright pink umbels of *Chaerophyllum hirsutum* 'Roseum'.   —*LH*

Oxalis adenophylla

Oxalis is a genus of some 700 species of fibrous-rooted, bulbous, rhizomatous, or tuberous annuals and perennials. The leaves are usually palmately divided into three leaflets and resemble shamrocks. Some species have more than 20 leaflets. The bright green cloverlike leaves are a foil for the large leaves of hostas and the fine-textured foliage of ferns. *Oxalis adeno-*

phylla forms a carpet, topping out at 4 inches, with leaves that have from 9 to 20 leaflets. Single pale lavender-purple flowers appear in late spring.

NATIVE HABITAT Temperate regions in South America

HARDINESS ZONES 6 to 8

HOW TO GROW *Oxalis* prefers climates with distinct rainy and dry seasons, moderate winters, and cool summers. For best results, plant them in gritty, well-drained soil in full sun or partial shade. These plants appreciate summer moisture but will rot if left in standing water. In very wet areas grow them in very well drained soil in raised beds, rock gardens, or alpine houses.

CULTIVARS AND RELATED SPECIES A mat-forming perennial, *Oxalis acetosella* is a good groundcover in partial to full shade. The open-faced bright pink blooms appear in late spring. Zones 3

Growing at alpine levels in open stony places in its native range, *Oxalis adenophylla* is a suitable plant to grow in a rock or trough garden.

to 5. *O. oregana* is native to coastal forests from Washington to California and is more tolerant of wet conditions. The white, sometimes pink blooms are veined in lavender; plants grow to between 10 and 12 inches. Zones 7 to 9. *O. regnellii* has three triangular leaflets that are green to purple on top and deep purple underneath. Its flowers are usually pink and contrast well with the foliage. Zones 7 to 10.

COMPANION PLANTS *Oxalis adenophylla* is best grown in rock gardens, troughs, or alpine beds where it is possible to replicate conditions found in its native habitat high in the mountains of Chile and Argentina, where it grows in open, rocky ground. Rock penstemon (*Penstemon rupicola*), *Armeria caespitosa* (syn. *Armeria juniperifolia*), *Papaver alpinum,* ground-hugging sedums, and *Lewisia columbiana* are culturally compatible companions.   —LH

Puschkinia scilloides var. *libanotica*
Puschkinia is a charming, early bulb of diminutive stature that puts on a big show. The starry white flowers have sky-blue stripes down the center of each petal and emerge before the paired leaves, which begin to unfurl as the flower stalk elongates to 3 to 5 inches. The plants go dormant soon after the seeds ripen in early summer.

NATIVE HABITAT Moist meadows and scrub in Turkey

HARDINESS ZONES 3 to 8

HOW TO GROW Set the rounded, paper-coated white bulbs 2 to 3 inches below the surface of rich, evenly moist soil in a spot with full to partial shade. Plants generously self-sow, and they can also be increased by offsets.

CULTIVARS AND RELATED SPECIES *Puschkinia scilloides* var. *libanotica* 'Alba' has white flowers. Zones 3 to 8.

Increasing by seed as well as offsets, tiny puschkinias spread to form a charming drift among taller bulbs.

COMPANION PLANTS In time, a dozen bulbs will multiply and spread to form a lovely drift among the stems of taller bulbs such as daffodils (*Narcissus*) and tulips, accented by the emerging pink noses of variegated Solomon's seal (*Polygonatum odoratum* 'Variegatum') and unfurling fern fronds. Use them in rock gardens or as a mass under shrubs.   —*CB*

Romulea bulbocodium

The showy, funnel-shaped, satiny-violet, lilac, pink, yellow, orange, or white flowers of *Romulea bulbocodium* have an egg-yolk-yellow throat. This is the most widely grown of a genus characterized by colorful, crocuslike flowers with recurved tips that open at midday and close again in the evening. Each corm produces six upright, threadlike basal leaves. They are more tender than their crocus relatives and are best grown under glass or in a hot, sunny rock garden.

NATIVE HABITAT Europe, Mediterranean, South and North Africa

HARDINESS ZONES 8 to 10

HOW TO GROW If you plan to grow these bulbs in a rock garden, plant seedlings out in mid-spring in a raised bed in well-drained, moderately fertile soil amended with grit. They are good subjects for a cool greenhouse or an alpine house. Increase them by division; plants also set seed, which you can collect and sow in compost in the greenhouse.

CULTIVARS AND RELATED SPECIES *Romulea bulbocodium* var. *clusiana* has a yellow throat and deep lilac petals. *R. crocea* is completely yellow. *R. nivalis* opens white with a sunny-yellow throat and purple reverse. It is hardier than some of the species and is worthy of a trial in a sunny rock garden. All are hardy in Zones 8 to 10.

COMPANION PLANTS Pair with low groundcovers including sedums, *Campanula* 'Elizabeth Oliver', and *Veronica liwanensis*.   —*LH*

Sanguinaria canadensis
BLOODROOT
Bloodroot spreads its pristine white stars in the early spring garden when few other native wildflowers are stirring. This showy woodland plant emerges with a single, deeply lobed leaf wrapped around the single flower bud. Each flower has 8 to 11 narrow petals surrounding a cluster of yellow stamens. Plants grow from a thick creeping rhizome that produces a bright orange sap for which the plant is named. An extract of bloodroot is an important anti-plaque

Unlike many bulb plants, North American native bloodroot keeps its leaves through the summer.

agent sometimes used in toothpaste and mouthwashes.

NATIVE HABITAT Deciduous woods, coves, floodplains, and rocky slopes from Nova Scotia and Manitoba south to Florida and Oklahoma

HARDINESS ZONES 3 to 9

HOW TO GROW Plant bloodroot in moist, humus-rich soil in light to full shade. Spring sun is important, but summer shade is essential. Unlike many bulbous plants, the leaves of bloodroot persist through the summer, but plants may go dormant with no ill effect during prolonged dry spells. They form dense clumps that can be divided in fall. Self-sown seedlings will appear, and plants reach flowering size in two to three years.

CULTIVARS AND RELATED SPECIES *Sanguinaria canadensis* 'Multiplex' is a stunning, fully double form with long-lasting flowers and huge, thick leaves. Plants must be divided every two to three years as rhizomes quickly become entangled and may start to rot, destroying the plants.

COMPANION PLANTS Combine bloodroot with wood anemone (*Anemone nemorosa*), spring-beauty (*Claytonia*), merrybells (*Uvularia*), Virginia bluebell (*Mertensia virginica*), and ferns. Spring bulbs, hostas, and primroses (*Primula*) are also good companions. Planted as a groundcover under shrubs and flowering trees bloodroot blossoms give the illusion of snow in the spring garden for the few glorious days they are in bloom. —*CB*

Scilla siberica
SIBERIAN SQUILL
The intense, almost iridescent, sapphire-blue bells of Siberian squill proclaim the onset of spring in no uncertain terms. Flowers on all species are bell-

Thriving in full sun or partial shade, Siberian squill does well in the open or under deciduous trees as long as it receives full sun during the spring growing season.

or star-shaped, usually blue, although white, pink, and lavender-purple varieties are available. Each flower, borne in terminal racemes on 6-inch stems, has six split tepals. Plants produce sparse, grasslike to rounded basal leaves.

NATIVE HABITAT Spring-blooming species are native to cold winter regions in Europe and Asia

HARDINESS ZONES 4 to 8

HOW TO GROW Siberian squill is easy to grow, thriving in full sun or partial shade, either in the open or under deciduous trees that receive full sun during the spring growing season. In fall, plant bulbs 3 to 4 inches deep in average, well-drained soil. Mass them in drifts for maximum effect, place them in clumps near walkways with other spring-blooming bulbs, or dot them through mixed borders. Plants

self-sow and naturalize easily but aren't aggressive. Separate offsets and seedlings in early summer as the leaves wither and die back. You can also divide clumps at this time.

CULTIVARS AND RELATED SPECIES
Scilla bifolia, or twin-leaf squill, presents its open, starry, lavender-blue flowers in one-sided racemes on 6-inch stems. Zones 4 to 8. *S. peruviana,* native to the Mediterranean, produces strappy green foliage in fall and stunning flowers in spring that each bear up to 100 luminous blue stars in a rounded raceme. It's best planted in soils that have perfect drainage and are amended with grit, or in pots. Zones 8 to 9.

COMPANION PLANTS The sky-blue flowers are a welcome contrast to white-blooming hellebores and the silvery-spotted, newly emerging foliage of lungwort (*Pulmonaria*). Plant them at the top of a wall with snowdrops (*Galanthus*) and early-blooming crocuses, where you can appreciate their virtues at close range. Large pools of squill bask in the luminous light of yellow forsythia and winter hazel (*Corylopsis spicata*).   —*LH*

Tecophilaea (or Tecophilea) cyanocrocus
CHILEAN BLUE CROCUS

Chilean blue crocus is a collector's plant of legendary acclaim. It is recognized by bulb aficionados the world over for its incredible funnel-shaped cerulean-blue flowers displayed on 6-inch stems above grasslike basal leaves.

NATIVE HABITAT Subalpine grasslands in South America. Botanists believe that it is now extinct in the wild.

HARDINESS ZONES 9 to 12

HOW TO GROW If you live in an area where it never freezes, you can grow Chilean blue crocus in raised or alpine beds; in colder regions cultivate them in a bulb frame, cool greenhouse, or alpine house. Plant corms 2 inches deep in fertile potting mix amended with grit or sharp sand. Keep bulbs cool until the first growth appears in late winter. Water them while they are in active growth, gradually reducing the amount of water as the bulbs go dormant after flowering and letting them dry out completely. Propagate from fresh seed sown in the fall in a fast-draining seed mix. For more information on threatened bulbs and bulb conservation, see "Buyer Beware," on page 14.

CULTIVARS AND RELATED SPECIES *Tecophilaea cyanocrocus* 'Leichtlinii' has sky-blue flowers with a white eye.

The flower of *T. cyanocrocus* var. *violacea* is more violet than blue.

COMPANION PLANTS This plant is too valuable to be grown outside except in its native range. It is usually cultivated as a specimen plant in a pot or on its own in an alpine bed.   —*LH*

Trillium species
WAKE ROBIN

The single flowers of wake robins are composed of three showy petals and three green sepals held erect at the top of 1- to 1½-foot stems above a whorl of bright green, broadly oval leaves. The genus *Trillium* is actually named for the triads of leaves, petals, and sepals. There are two distinctive growth forms: The sessile species have stalkless flowers borne erect on top of the foliage. In the pedicellate species, the flowers are carried above the leaves on stalks. Plants grow from thick rhizomes with fleshy roots.

NATIVE HABITAT Rich deciduous woods, rocky slopes, and floodplains from Quebec and Minnesota south to Georgia and Indiana

HARDINESS ZONES 3 to 8

HOW TO GROW Plant in humus-rich, moist soil in light to partial shade. Plants form multistemmed clumps from buds on the rhizomes. If the soil stays moist, the foliage persists through the summer. Plants may form offsets and can be divided after a few years. Propagation by seed is slow, but self-sown seedlings will reach flowering age in five to seven years. The sessile trilliums develop more quickly from seed. Proceed with care when you purchase this native plant: Many *Trillium* species sold today are collected from the wild. Be sure to buy only nursery-propagated stock from reputable dealers. Avoid plants labeled "nursery-grown" (as opposed to "nursery propagated"), since these may be wild-collected. For more information on the problems of wild collection and what to look for when purchasing bulbs, see "Buyer Beware," on page 14.

CULTIVARS AND RELATED SPECIES
Trillium grandiflorum 'Flore-Pleno' is a rare and enchantingly beautiful fully double form. 'Snow Bunting' is a large-flowered white double. *T. cuneatum,* toad trillium, takes its name from the brown-and-green-mottled leaves resembling the back of a toad. The sweet fruit-scented, deep maroon 2½-inch flowers are sessile, and stick straight up from the leaves. Plants grow up to a foot high and may go dormant after flowering. Zones 4 to 8. *T. erectum*, red trillium, or stinking benjamin, produces a broad ring of wide leaves on 1- to 2-foot stems adorned by 1-inch deep-blood-red flowers that nod

slightly on 1- to 4-inch stalks. The name stinking benjamin makes reference to the plant's ill scent, which is reminiscent of a wet dog. Zones 4 to 9. *T. flexipes*, bent trillium, has creamy-white flowers that droop or stand erect on 1- to 4-inch stalks. Broad leaves top 1- to 2-foot stems borne two or more to a clump. Zones 3 to 8. *T. kurabayashii* is a stunning huge sessile species from the West coast with a large whorl of mottled leaves and deep wine-red flowers atop 2-foot stalks. Zones 6 to 8. *T. luteum,* yellow trillium, is nearly identical to *T. cuneatum* in all respects except that the flowers are chartreuse to lemon-yellow and smell of lemons. Zones 4 to 8. *T. sulcatum* is a robust species with large maroon flowers held above the bold leaves. Mature plants reach 3 feet, and many color variants from white and yellow to bicolor are found in the wild. Zones 4 to 9.

COMPANION PLANTS Trilliums are a welcome addition to any shade or woodland garden with wildflowers, perennials, sedges, and ferns. They are lovely planted with bulbs, spring-blooming shrubs, and trees.　　—*CB*

Triteleia laxa
ITHURIEL'S SPEAR, FOOL'S ONION, GRASS NUT, PRETTY FACE
Triteleia laxa blooms in shades ranging from pale lavender to deeper purple. Its long, grasslike basal foliage withers and dies back as the blooms appear. The loosely arranged umbels of 20 to 25 funnel-shaped flowers on 18-inch stalks look very much like the flowers of ornamental onions (*Allium*). The genus *Triteleia* comprises some

Native to deciduous woods, trilliums thrive in moist, humus-rich soil in light to partial shade. This is red trillium.

In western North America where it is native, Ithuriel's spear naturalizes easily by self-sowing. This is 'Queen Fabiola'.

large violet flowers on 2½-foot stems. *T. ixioides*, known as pretty face or golden star, produces yellow flowers with a purple stripe and veining.

COMPANION PLANTS Along the edge of a woodland or in a partially shady border, the rounded umbels of Ithuriel's spear are complemented by the cheerful yellow daisylike flowers of leopard's bane (*Doronicum* 'Magnificum') and columbine (*Aquilegia*).   —LH

Tulipa
HYBRID TULIPS

Hybrid tulips are the party girls of the bulb world. Throughout the spring they parade around in an array of colors and forms. Blooms range from goblet- and bowl-shaped to lily-shaped, star-shaped, and doubles. Flowers are composed of six tepals (sepals and petals) and can be smooth, fringed, wavy, or ruffled. Tulips come in all shades of the color wheel except for true blue. The basal foliage is usually mid- to gray-green and long oval in shape. The genus includes more than 100 species and hundreds of named cultivars, which have been classified into 15 categories based on flowering time and tepal characteristics. By choosing varieties that bloom at different times it is possible to have a three-month succession of flower.

NATIVE HABITAT Garden hybrids

HARDINESS ZONES 3 to 8

HOW TO GROW Rich, well-drained soil is essential for tulips to perform. Work the soil to a depth of at least 12 inches and add well-rotted compost or leaf mold. Tulips are heavy feeders

15 species of cormous perennials, which are very similar to the closely related plants in the genus *Brodiaea*.

NATIVE HABITAT Western North America

HARDINESS ZONES 6 to 10

HOW TO GROW Plant corms in autumn 3 to 4 inches deep in well-drained, rich soil in a spot that is in full sun or partial shade. They are best planted in groups of 6 to 9 spaced 3 to 4 inches apart. Ithuriel's spears thrive with even moisture while growing but can't tolerate much water once dormant. Apply winter mulch in areas where they might be less hardy. In areas with summer rain, tuck them into a rock garden or raised beds. In western North America they naturalize easily by self-sowing. Propagate by separating offsets or dividing clumps when plants are dormant.

CULTIVARS AND RELATED SPECIES
Triteleia laxa 'Queen Fabiola' displays

By choosing tulip varieties that bloom at different times, it is possible to have a three-month succession of flowers. Above is 'Ollioules'.

and benefit from an application of well-balanced organic fertilizer. For best results place them where they receive a minimum of 5 or 6 hours of sun. Plant in the fall 5 to 6 inches deep if grown as annuals and several inches deeper if grown as perennials. Space bulbs 4 to 6 inches apart, in groups of 6 to 9, for maximum impact. Unfortunately, tulips are a preferred food for deer, rabbits, voles, and chipmunks. In some locations it may be necessary to top-dress the area where tulips have been planted with sharp grit or gravel to help fend off rodents. After the blooms have faded, deadhead to prevent seed formation, but let the leaves wither and turn yellow before removing them.

CULTIVARS AND RELATED SPECIES

Tulipa 'Apricot Beauty' is a single, early tulip that blooms in mid-spring with fragrant cup-shaped salmon flow-ers on 14-inch stems. 'Barcelona' is classified as a triumph tulip and presents fuchsia-purple flowers. It blooms in mid-spring on 14- to 20-inch stems and is good for forcing and use in pots. 'Ollioules', a Darwin hybrid, is a large, much-favored old cultivar that is dark rose edged in a sheen of silver. Darwin hybrids are good naturalizers. 'White Triumphator' has ivory goblet-shaped flowers with pointed tips and is known as a lily-flowered tulip. 'Blue Parrot', an oldie with violet-blue flow-ers, is a showstopper. Parrot tulips have large, irregularly cut tepals that curl and twist and are wonderful for flower arranging.

COMPANION PLANTS You can bed out hybrid tulips in mass plantings to great effect or intersperse clusters of tulips in perennial beds and borders, in the rock garden, or in containers. With such a wide range of colors, pair hot-pink and purple or red and purple for high impact, or use soft pastels together for a more harmonious effect. —*LH*

Tulipa species
TULIP

Most species tulips are smaller and more delicate and graceful than their hybrid progeny, but they display the same sumptuous range of flower color.

NATIVE HABITAT Areas with dry summers and cool winters in central Asia

HARDINESS ZONES 3 to 8

HOW TO GROW See the growing information for hybrid tulips, above. You can also grow smaller species tulips in rock gardens, bulb frames, alpine houses, and containers.

CULTIVARS AND RELATED SPECIES The primrose-yellow flowers of *Tulipa batalinii* shine in a rock garden or nestled among pavers in a walkway. Plants are 4 to 6 inches tall and can be perennialized. *T. clusiana* shows off its white flowers on slim, graceful 12-inch stems. You can easily identify *T. greigii* by its splotched or purple-black-striped leaves. It bears fire-engine-red, bowl-shaped flowers with black throats on 10- to 16-inch stems. Cultivars range in color from white to pink and yellow. *T. humilis*, a diminutive species at 4 to 6 inches, bears open-faced starry rose-pink flowers with a yellow base. Cultivars are scarlet, purple, and magenta. All are hardy in Zones 3 to 8.

COMPANION PLANTS Drifts of species tulips light up the ground when planted among navelwort (*Omphalodes cappadocica* 'Starry Eyes'), dog-tooth violet (*Erythronium revolutum*), and spring vetchling (*Lathyrus vernus*). —*LH*

Most species tulips are more delicate and graceful than their hybrid offspring yet display the same wide range of colors. Above is diminutive *Tulipa humilis* 'Persian Pearl'.

With sufficient moisture, the foliage of native atamasco lily persists in summer. If it gets too dry, the plant goes dormant.

Zephyranthes atamasca
ATAMASCO LILY

Atamasco lilies have the uncanny habit of springing into bloom soon after seasonal rains return, almost as if appearing by magic. The 3-inch, snow-white flowers of atamasco lily are carried above the new leaves from early spring to early summer. The narrow 1-foot strap-shaped leaves grow from true bulbs and persist all summer if sufficient moisture is available. Plants go dormant during drought.

NATIVE HABITAT Low pine woods, meadows, marshes, and roadside ditches of the coastal plain from Virginia to Alabama

HARDINESS ZONES 6 to 10

HOW TO GROW Plant in rich, moist to seasonally wet, acidic soil in full sun or light shade. Plants will grow in shallow water if planted in light soil. Divide bulbs after flowering if they become so congested that flowering wanes. Self-sown seedlings will appear, but they develop slowly.

CULTIVARS AND RELATED SPECIES *Hymenocallis occidentalis,* spider lily, also in the amaryllis family, is a showy plant with straplike leaves wider toward the tips and clusters of spidery white flowers with six slender segments and a central, circular membrane that lies over the segments. The fragrant flowers are borne on 2-foot stalks in late spring and summer. Zones 7 to 10.

COMPANION PLANTS Atamasco lilies look best planted in great sweeps. Where they are happy, they will increase rapidly, so you can start with a dozen or so bulbs. Combine the snowy chalices with spike rush (*Juncus*), sedges, and camass (*Camassia scilloides*). Choose cardinal flower (*Lobelia cardinalis*) and ferns for interest later in the season. Grown in pots, atamasco lilies add a touch of class to water gardens.   —*CB*

USDA Hardiness Zone Map

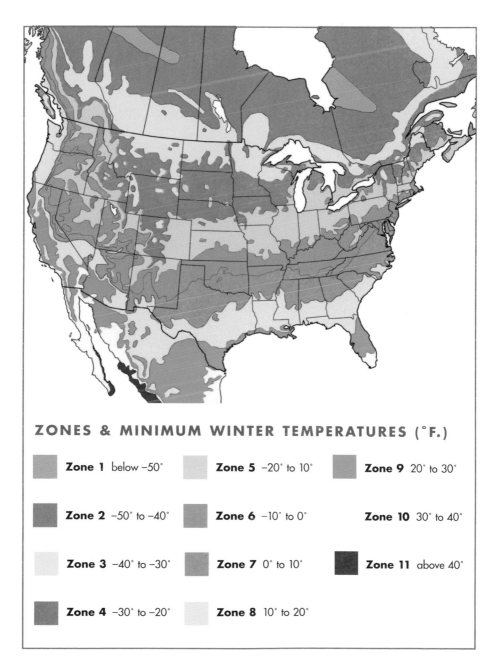

ZONES & MINIMUM WINTER TEMPERATURES (°F.)

Zone 1 below –50°

Zone 2 –50° to –40°

Zone 3 –40° to –30°

Zone 4 –30° to –20°

Zone 5 –20° to 10°

Zone 6 –10° to 0°

Zone 7 0° to 10°

Zone 8 10° to 20°

Zone 9 20° to 30°

Zone 10 30° to 40°

Zone 11 above 40°

For More Information

The Complete Book of Bulbs, Corms, Tubers, and Rhizomes: A Step-by-Step Guide to Nature's Easiest and Most Rewarding Plants
Brian Mathew and Philip Swindells
Reader's Digest, 1994

Growing Bulbs: The Complete Practical Guide
Brian Mathew
Timber Press, 1997

Adventures With Hardy Bulbs
Louise Beebe Wilder
Lyons Press, 1998

Bulbs (Revised, expanded)
John E. Bryan
Timber Press, 2002

Bulbs
Roger Phillips and Martyn Rix
Pan, 1989, Paperback
(Random House edition is out of print; this is the British edition available from Amazon.com.uk)

Bulbs for the Rock Garden
Jack Elliott
Timber Press, 1996

Bulbs of North America: North American Rock Garden Society
Mary Jane McGary (Editor)
Timber Press and North American Rock Garden Society, 2001

Daffodils for American Gardens
(Revised and Updated)
Brent Heath and Becky Heath
Bright Sky Press, 2001

Gardener's Guide to Growing Lilies
Michael Jefferson-Brown and Harris Howland
Timber Press, 2002

The Little Bulbs: A Tale of Two Gardens
Elizabeth Lawrence, Introduction by Allen Lacy
Duke University Press, 1986

Naturalizing Bulbs
Rob Proctor
Henry Holt & Company, 1997

The Plantfinder's Guide to Early Bulbs
Rod Leeds
Timber Press, 2000

The Tulip: The Story of a Flower That Has Made Men Mad
Anna Pavord
Bloomsbury Publishing, 2001

Tulipomania: The Story of the World's Most Coveted Flower and the Extraordinary Passions It Aroused
Mike Dash
Three Rivers Press, 2001

Tulips for American Gardens
Brent Heath and Becky Heath
Bright Sky Press, 2001

Mail-Order Sources

ARROWHEAD ALPINES
P.O. Box 857
Fowlerville, MI 48836
517-223-3581
www.arrowhead-alpines.com

BRENT AND BECKY'S BULBS
7463 Heath Trail
Gloucester, VA 23061
804-693-3966
www.brentandbeckysbulbs.com

DUTCH GARDENS
144 Intervale Road
Burlington, VT 05401
800-944-2250
www.dutchgardens.com

JOHN SCHEEPERS
P.O. Box 638
Bantam, CT 06750
860-567-0838
www.johnscheepers.com

McCLURE & ZIMMERMAN
P.O. Box 368
Friesland, WI 53935
800-883-6998
www.mzbulb.com

MESSELAAR BULB CO.
P.O. Box 269
Ipswich, MA 01938
978-356-3737
www.tulipbulbs.com

ODYSSEY BULBS
8984 Meadow Lane
Berrien Springs, MI 49103
877-220-1651
www.odysseybulbs.com

OLD HOUSE GARDENS
536 West Third Street
Ann Arbor, MI 48103
734-995-1486
www.oldhousegardens.com
(Heirloom bulbs)

SENECA HILL PERENNIALS
3712 County Route 57
Oswego, NY 13126
315-342-5915
www.senecahill.com

THE TEMPLE NURSERY
H. Lyman
Box 591
Trumansburg, NY 14886
(Snowdrops in the green only; no phone
orders; no web site)

VAN BOURGONDIEN
P.O. Box 1000
Babylon, NY 11702
800-622-9997
www.dutchbulbs.com

WAYSIDE GARDENS
1 Garden Lane
Hodges, SC 29695
800-213-0379
www.waysidegardens.com

Pest and Disease Control Sources

The companies listed below offer a wide range of the least toxic treatment options available to deal with a pest infestation or plant disease that may crop up in your garden. Explore the products and treatment approaches developed by companies such as these. They are sound alternatives to many of the highly toxic chemicals commonly found on the shelves of garden centers and hardware stores. No matter where you shop, be sure to read labels and find out as much as you can about a product before you apply it in your garden.

GARDENS ALIVE
5100 Schenley Place
Lawrenceburg, IN 47025
812-537-8650
www.gardensalive.com
(horticultural oils, botanical pesticides,
beneficial organisms)

ARBICO ENVIRONMENTALS
P.O. Box 8910
Tucson, AZ 85738
800-827-2847
www.arbico.com
(beneficial organisms, pest repellents,
physical controls, soil amendments,
cover crops)

RINCON-VITOVA INSECTARIES
P.O. Box 1555
Ventura, CA 93002
800-248-2847
www.rinconvitova.com
(beneficial organisms)

Contributors

C. COLSTON BURRELL is an avid plantsman, garden designer, and award-winning author. His books include *Perennials for Today's Gardens* (Meredith, 2000); *Perennial Combinations* (Rodale, 1999), a Garden Book Club bestseller; and *A Gardener's Encyclopedia of Wildflowers* (Rodale, 1997). He is the author of the Brooklyn Botanic Garden handbook *The Sunny Border* (2002) and the editor of several others, most recently *Wildflower Gardens* (1999) and *The Shady Border* (1998). He gardens on ten acres in the Blue Ridge Mountains of Virginia.

ALESSANDRO CHIARI has been the plant propagator at Brooklyn Botanic Garden since 1998. He studied tropical agriculture at the University of Florence, Italy, and plant science at the University of Connecticut, and he has worked as a horticulturist in Zambia, Paraguay, Chile, and Peru.

MARK FISHER has been with Brooklyn Botanic Garden since 1984, when he started work as an instructor in the Education Greenhouses. The following year he became the curator of the Desert House. Since 1996, Fisher has been the foreman of the Steinhardt Conservatory. He holds a B.S. in ornamental horticulture from Colorado State University and has a lifelong interest in gardening and growing bulbs.

BETH HANSON is former managing editor of Brooklyn Botanic Garden's 21st Century Gardening Series. She is the editor of the BBG handbooks *Summer-Blooming Bulbs* (2001), *Gourmet Herbs* (2001), *Natural Disease Control* (2000), *Chile Peppers* (1999), and *Easy Compost* (1997), and contributed to BBG's *Gardener's Desk Reference* (Henry Holt, 1998). She lives outside New York City and writes about gardening, health, and the environment for various publications.

LUCY HARDIMAN is the owner of Perennial Partners, a Portland garden-design firm. She also lectures locally and nationally, and her garden writing and photography have appeared in both local and national garden publications.

SCOTT KUNST is the owner of Old House Gardens, the world's only mail-order source devoted entirely to heirloom bulbs. With a small crew of dedicated enthusiasts, he searches the globe for spectacular old bulbs that are in danger of extinction and then works with small farmers to propagate and offer them through his catalog and web site to gardeners across the United States. A landscape historian and popular lecturer, Kunst gardens in the historic Old West Side neighborhood of Ann Arbor, Michigan.

KATIE STANNARD is vice president for bulbs at Old House Gardens. She is a master gardener and holds a B.A. from Carleton College and an M.A. from Carnegie Mellon University. She confesses to a small addiction to hyacinths, double daffodils, and cannas.

MARK C. TEBBITT, PH.D. is a botanist who specializes in cultivated plant taxonomy. He is currently head of the Horticultural Taxonomy Department at Brooklyn Botanic Garden. Previously he worked at the Royal Botanic Garden, Edinburgh, on the European Garden Flora project and at the University of Glasgow on the taxonomy of orchids. He has given talks and published papers on several aspects of horticultural taxonomy and botany and has conducted botanical field-work around the world. Since he was a child he has been an avid grower of all types of plants. He is currently researching a book on begonias.

Photos
ALAN & LINDA DETRICK cover, pages 7 top, 13, 16, 43, 56, 63, 65, 67, 68, 69, 84, 85, 88, 92, 96
DAVID CAVAGNARO pages 1, 6, 7 bottom, 11, 22, 26, 30, 31 both, 32, 33 right, 46, 52, 57, 66, 73, 77, 78, 81, 86, 89, 93, 94, 99
CHARLES MARDEN FITCH pages 4, 8, 10, 54, 79, 87, 91, 97
DEREK FELL pages 15, 21, 34, 38, 58, 59, 71
SCOTT KUNST pages 18 both, 24, 25, 40, 41, 42 both
NEIL SODERSTROM pages 20, 45, 55, 83, 98
JERRY PAVIA pages 28, 36, 74, 80, 82, 90
C. COLSTON BURRELL pages 33 left, 64, 70, 76, 100
ALESSANDRO CHIARI page 44 both
BRENT & BECKY HEATH pages 60, 61, 62
VAN BOURGONDIEN page 63

Index

BROOKLYN BOTANIC GARDEN

MICHAEL FUSCO

World renowned for pioneering gardening information, Brooklyn Botanic Garden's 21st-Century Gardening Series of award-winning guides provides spectacularly photographed, compact, practical advice for gardeners in every region of North America.

Join Brooklyn Botanic Garden as an annual Subscriber Member and receive four gardening handbooks, delivered directly to you, each year. Other benefits include free admission to many gardens across the country, plus four issues of *Plants & Gardens News, Members News,* and our guide to courses and public programs.

For additional information on Brooklyn Botanic Garden, including other membership packages, call 718-623-7210 or visit our web site at www.bbg.org. To order other fine titles published by BBG, call 718-623-7286, or shop in our online store at www.bbg.org/gardenemporium.

**MORE BOOKS ON
GARDENING WITH BULBS**